ONE FOOT
IN THE DOOR

This book is dedicated to my Sister, Alison; to my son, Ben; to my daughter, Layla; to my stepsons, Christian, Francois and Aaron and to all their respective families. And to anyone who may be interested.

ACKNOWLEDGEMENTS

To my parents, Fred and Pidge for giving me the opportunity to be. To all those who have given me the chance to learn, knowingly or unknowingly. To Emma, a really close friend, who recently lost her courageous struggle against a rare cancer and who helped with much of the research for this book and who was consistently encouraging when I was doubting my progress. To Steve Taylor and Iain Scott, for permission to quote from their respective books. To Fliss, for conscientiously checking grammar, punctuation and spelling. To Viva! for checking animal husbandry facts. To all those throughout history who have suffered and are continuing to do so because of our immaturity as a species. To all those throughout history who have tried their best to make this planet a better place to live, whether through politics, art, literature, science, practical and caring work or more recently environmental concerns. To Iain and Becky for all their non-selfish work.

Design by Christian Nouyou.
Printed in Wales by Gomer Press.

First published in 2024 by Mike Dodd in a limited edition of 500, each signed by the author.

ISBN 978-1-915188-21-2

At least 50% of the profit from sales of this book will go to The Wildlife For All Trust.

ONE FOOT
IN THE DOOR

Mike Dodd

Contents

Introduction

My dear mother was diagnosed with pancreatic cancer in May 1994 and died on November the 5th in the same year. She was 78. By her bed, in a small notebook, she had started to describe her early teenage years. She'd written only 4 pages. Clearly things had not been easy for her as she'd missed much of her schooling looking after her seriously asthmatic mother. It was interesting and well written and left my sister and I wanting to know more. I don't know why she stopped writing but brief as it was it was lovely to get an insight into her early life, a time she'd never opened up about while she was still with us. But it wasn't until lockdown in the winter of 2020 when many were dying in the first phase of COVID, that my thoughts returned to my mother's death and her little notebook. I began to wonder if there was anything worthwhile in my experience that may be helpful and useful to pass on to my children, their families and anyone else who may be interested.

I started to recall a powerful experience I'd had in my 30th year, an experience of varying intensity lasting about 3 days. At around the same time a group of friends who were compiling a record of similar experiences helped to focus my attention. Depending on ones culture these experiences have been given various names, the best known of which are, salvation, enlightenment, oceanic, satori [zen], and oneness. Names which have, perhaps, become overly charged through time with many grandiose and romanticised historical references. My preference is for the appropriately descriptive word 'oneness', the reason for which will be expanded upon in a later chapter.

As I recalled the experience, something I hadn't done with any serious intent over many years, I was surprised at the extraordinary clarity of my memory given that it happened 47 years ago. Back then I had read about the breakthrough experiences of the Zen masters and the enlightenment of the Buddha but I'd never come across anyone who had experienced such or something similar. Although I didn't know who to talk to about it, I did contact Christmas Humphries, whom I knew from the Buddhist Society in London and he asked me to travel up to see him but, for one reason or another, I didn't go.

It is clear that our present consciousness mindset or paradigm is stuck, expressed sometimes as 'you can't change human nature'. If that is true, notwithstanding our kinder tendencies, then our often disruptive and immature behaviour towards each other and the rest of the living world will continue to manifest. We will continue to act like a thoughtless virus infecting our host, in this case our beautiful earth, without a care, the consequences of which are all too evident.

So, my intention is to describe the lead up to the 'oneness experience' and then the experience itself and what that experience might imply. The implications of such an experience are potentially massive. Questions will arise which challenge many 'sacred cows' [definition, an institution or custom that is so venerated that it is above criticism]. In these challenging times, I'm hoping that this book will provide encouragement to think and question more deeply as new solutions to personal, social, economic and global issues, with some notable exceptions, are not forthcoming, or at least are not being approached with the urgency required.

Recognising the need for change, there are many individuals and groups who are attempting to create a better world through nature conservation, scientific endeavour and community projects, but adding a small amount of yellow into a sea of blue doesn't turn it green. A good friend of mine when asked 'Surely if everyone does their little bit...' quickly interjected and replied 'Then only a little bit gets done'. Our present psychological paradigm often thwarts well intentioned projects because of our powerful conditioning within what I call the 'you *or* me' world.

Over the long arc of time, humans have achieved extraordinary things in their expressions of creativity whether in various forms of art, in tool making, architecture, husbandry, textiles, literature and latterly in science etc. but we are also too easily persuaded to act in appalling ways through the exercise of power over others, religious extremism, wars, abuse of each other and nature, the profligate use of Earth's resources and so on. No one can be blamed for our present condition; it is simply the way we have so far evolved. That doesn't mean it has to stay that way. My experience indicated a different potential, a fuller evolution, a fuller consciousness.

I need to make it clear that I'm writing from 'normal' consciousness as the oneness experience didn't last that long. However, for that short duration there was a radical shift in perception and understanding. I feel very fortunate to have put my foot in the door of a new reality, a reality that felt open hearted, complete and undivided, clearly a potential within each of us.

Language provides us with a means of understanding the world and through words, we have created platforms for that understanding. Passionate conversation throws ideas into the vast pool of knowledge, often improving and shifting perceptions and positions, slowly rippling through and advancing humanity in its search for deeper comprehension or meaning. My 'experience' and it's implications may be helpful in realising a more developed attitude to each other, all other life forms and this wonderful planet. So, I'm throwing this contribution into the mix in an attempt to add to the quest for an evolution to a greater maturity in behaviour, attitudes, understanding and action.

1
An Awakening Interest

I don't quite know how but in 1962 I gained entry to Cambridge's prestigious university to study medicine. It was dependent on an extra chemistry exam which I managed to pass after the summer spent at a 'crammer' in London. I didn't think my interview with the Dean of Emmanuel College had gone very well as halfway through the interview when I'd answered some preliminary questions, the Dean nodded off. At school we'd been briefed on various scenarios which might arise during interviews, but nodding off was not one of them. Was he bored or tired or had he imbibed too many glasses of port at lunch? Admittedly I'd seen him at a distance having lunch at the staff table, bottles visible, in the college's refectory just before my allotted interview time. A few awkward and indecisive moments passed before I decided I should attempt to wake him up. But just as I was reaching forward to tap him on the knee, his eyelids wearily opened. And from his imposing leather brass studded chair, he straightened himself up from his sleepy and slumped position, slowly reanimating his unshaven face, and the interview continued.

Not long after I'd arrived to take up residence in the town, I decided to familiarise myself with the place, its buildings, bars, cinemas and shops, etc. Not far from the impressive landmark of Kings College Chapel I passed a lamppost sporting a poster advertising a talk by the Rev. Ananda Bodhi, followed by, and this was the bit that intrigued me, ex Baptist minister! I have to admit, I was shocked. The idea that anyone could change their religion had never occurred to me before. It was a no brainer, I had to attend. It was a small lecture hall, in I forget which College, with sloping seats down to an impressive quartered oak table where there was seated, in the recognisable orange robe, a Buddhist monk. What he talked about was, I thought, very different to the tedious and sometimes sanctimonious sermons I'd become accustomed to at the compulsory Sunday church attendances at school. Although I can't recall anything he said, I do remember being impressed. A question-and-answer session followed and although I don't remember the question I asked, his reply was wonderfully unexpected. Why he considered that throwing a piece of chalk at me was an appropriate answer, I'm not sure but in the heady intellectual atmosphere of an esteemed university I was fascinated by this seemingly absurd response. I wanted to know more.

Over the next few years, I found various books browsing the second-hand section of a local bookshop. I found 'First and Last Freedom' by J. Krishnamurti, a well-known Indian teacher. His beginnings were extraordinary. He was discovered playing with his brother on a beach in India by a character called Bishop Leadbetter of the Theosophists, a group headed at that time by Annie Besant. For some inexplicable reason the Bishop was convinced that this young boy was going to be the next Messiah! After some legal haggling, arrangements were made for the two brothers to travel to England and be privately tutored.

Much later when Krishnamurti was in his late twenties, the Order of the Star, the organisation the Theosophists had created to promote him as the coming Messiah, was ready to present him to a large, excited gathering of followers at Ommen in Holland. To everyone's surprise and shock, Krishnamurti stood up and in a remarkable speech, rejected the title, essentially saying that truth cannot be organised and that he wasn't interested in having followers. Apart from a small stipend, he gave back donated money and properties and said he would continue to talk to anyone who was interested to hear him.

At around the same time I came across a delightful, if over romanticised little book of the life of the Buddha, 'The Light of Asia' written as a poem, by one of England's first Buddhists, Sir Edwin Arnold. It tells the story of the Buddha's early life as a privileged prince who was unaware of suffering and death, until, one day he ventured out into the 'normal' life of the local people. He was shocked to the core at the suffering he witnessed and determined to understand the cause. He sought out various spiritual teachers none of whom, it seems, were able to satisfactorily answer his insistent questions. Eventually, the story goes, he achieved, whilst meditating under the Bodhi tree, a state of enlightenment, a condition beyond psychological suffering. This he expressed as the 4 Noble truths, which, to précis are a] that suffering exists b] it has a cause c] it has an end and d] there is a way to bring about that end. This exploration formed the original basis of the popular non-theistic philosophy. From these beginnings and other influential books I realised that my thinking up until then had not been seriously challenged but cosily cocooned within a western and Christian mindset.

My continuing interest in pottery was fulfilled by frequent visits to the broad collection of pots, both European and Eastern, at the Fitzwilliam Museum. I strongly responded to the vitality of hand-made work, mostly pre-industrial country ware. Much of it moved me deeply. It was towards the end of my second year's study whilst walking to my favourite cafe, I was struck by the thought, quite out of the blue, 'I could be a potter!' The thought was such that all tension fell away, and a feeling of rightness remained. Up until that moment I'd ridden my life without any significant resistance but now I had to make a decision, a decision I didn't find difficult. I wrote to my parents quoting the Shakespearean 'to be or not to be' reason for my change of heart! My father, being a keen gardener, wrote back saying 'Camelia's don't grow in chalky ground, good luck', with the obvious implication that everyone needs to find the right ground in which to grow. I then set about applying to various London Art Colleges. I was accepted at Hammersmith for a 3-year course. I stayed a year, simply because the instruction was poor and didn't meet my desire to learn.

It was the sixties and there was much indiscipline amongst both students and lecturers with overlong, if enjoyable, forays to the pub. So, I took myself back home somewhat depressed at the way things had gone so far. But, at the same time I determined to set about visiting various rental properties that might be suitable for establishing a small pottery. After a few unsuccessful months my father heard of a couple of cottages for rent on a farm a few miles away.

One of them, a tiny exquisite 2 up, 2 down flint cottage, sheltering under the South Downs, sat in the middle of a small field in the village of Edburton, with plenty of room to build a studio and kiln. The rent was £2.50 a week. Perfect. The £90 I had in the bank at the time was sufficient to build a small lean-to workshop against the end wall of the cottage. The local power station in Shoreham was closing down so I was able to find enough used and unwanted fire bricks to build a two chambered wood fired kiln. As I stood back, hands on hips, to admire my own handiwork, the first chamber, slowly at first and then quite dramatically collapsed under the thrust of an unsupported arch. It was a steep learning curve. To earn my keep, I took a job as a thrower, a skill I'd learnt at school, at a rat-infested basement pottery in Croydon followed by a 6 month stint teaching pottery at a comprehensive school in Crawley, West Sussex.

At around about the same time I joined the Buddhist Society, located in Eccleston Square, London, a short walk from Victoria Station. Basil, a delightful man, was my Rinzai Zen meditation coach. The train timetable was such that I arrived a little late for my introductory class only to be greeted by the question 'What's the difference between East and West?' And on another occasion 'What's the distance between you and I?' At the time I was perplexed by such questions which, I learnt later, was the intention. They are examples of Zen Koans (mind confusing questions).

In the evenings I would read anything related to the mind. Western authors such as Jung, Freud, Maslow, Fechner and Fromm. Eastern books by

Ramana Maharishi, Krishnamurti, the Zen master Huang Po, Haiku poetry, in fact anything I could get my hands on including some spurious publications on the miraculous exploits of Tibetan monks! I also came across 'The Little Prince' by Antoine de Saint-Exupery, 'The Tao of Physics', 'Zen Catholicism', 'Zen and the Art of Motorcycle Maintenance', 'The Taboo Against Knowing Who You Are', by Alan Watts, and Richard Bach's 'Jonathan Livingston Seagull' and his 'The Adventures of a Reluctant Messiah' crossed my path. I loved this last little book as the author describes a garage mechanic who realises he's destined to become the next Messiah. In his reluctance to realise this expectancy, he decides to take people up in a small two-seater plane and when they ask him a question, he flips open his Messiah's handbook to find an answer. One passenger who complains that he is unable to do something is provided with this quote from the handbook 'Argue for your limitations, and sure enough they are yours'. Brilliant. A piece of advice I should have given more attention to. There were other books which I've long forgotten or relegated to second-hand book shops.

The Rinzai Zen meditation technique is very simple. Essentially you concentrate on the in breath and then the out breath, counting up to ten breaths. Then repeat. Naturally, particularly at the beginning, thoughts involuntarily intrude before you even reach five! If you are 'awake' you quickly realise their interference with your regime and you get back to counting. If not, your thoughts meander off in often weird directions. I can remember once being taken over by the random image of an aunt unwrapping a chocolate orange! It's called day dreaming, not very little different from night dreaming. Eventually you remember what you are supposed to be doing. It certainly made me aware of the vagaries of the mind and how little time we spend in the present moment. In fact, becoming aware that you are not aware, is awareness.

I thought at the time that the word meditation was too grand a description for what I considered to be a practise of concentration. But slowly, rather than watch the drifting thoughts appear, I began to question them, 'Why am I thinking that?' 'Who's in charge here, me or my thoughts?' 'Who am I?' And so on. One day, whilst trying to fix a shelf in the tiny cottage kitchen, it fell down, and I noticed annoyance, frustration and anger arise in me. I stopped and asked myself why. It was fairly obvious, clearly, I wanted the job to go smoothly as there were other things I needed or wanted to do. So, my want created frustration. Um, interesting. Gradually I noticed that I was made up of wants/desires, fears, hopes, regrets, defences and so on which I called later my 'me' or more scientifically, the acculturated self. At the time I thought of it as a lot of accumulated stuff analogous to the caddisfly larvae that surrounds and protects its soft and vulnerable body with detritus it finds on the bottom of a pond or river, little bits of wood and grains of sand etc. Another book, recommended to me, I think, by someone at the Buddhist Society was called 'Meditation and Concentration' and in the back of it were various quotations, two of which I paid particular attention to, 'Life is one' and 'You are not what you *think* you are, but what you think, you are'. I would take my Welsh sheepdog, Queenie, out for her daily walk and ask myself, what on Earth was meant by 'Life is one'? It seemed such a contradictory statement.

The questioning continued and since I didn't keep a diary at the time, the sequence of various insights remains vague, but the practise was going well and I was enjoying sitting down in spare moments between making pots and household chores and further examining what came up. Now there were much longer intervals between unwanted thoughts, and I started to feel a spatial quality of openness. There was a process of disidentification and unlearning going on. Noticing what was not relevant or necessary. Sometimes I felt an energetic expansiveness or a calm quietness. There was a sense that my 'me' was disappearing. I started to ask, 'So what is really happening here?' Ok, light travels into the eye and the brain picks up what it's reflected off. That happens whether you like it or not. So who sees? Is there simply seeing, or is the seeing coloured by the 'me'? So, is seeing contaminated by content? Perhaps contaminated is not the right word here, changed, distorted maybe? Why are there thoughts and emotions when unasked for? I was probing, looking for answers.

Life, as it does, continued and a friend from London informed me that there was a Zen master visiting who would be holding a sesshin (a meditation weekend) in Notting Hill Gate. I had read about the exploits of various Zen masters and was keen to know more. There were perhaps 50 people attending. The Master would occasionally stroll around the fidgety and sometimes sleepy meditators and would, if he felt you were losing awareness, strike you sharply on the back with a stick to wake you up! At the start you were told that you could ask a question of the Master by raising your hand. So I decided to take the opportunity, although looking back I'm not sure the question I asked was the best one. But it was related to my then enquiry into the nature of consciousness. So I asked 'Is consciousness itself an illusion?' The Zen master was nicknamed 'The Rock' I think because when he sat cross legged with his black robe extending out to the floor, he assumed a sort of blocky appearance. 'Yes,' he said making the gesture like the descending swish of a samurai sword 'You have to cut through, there are 8 levels'. He didn't speak a word of English, so this is what I understood from his interpreter. Whether the interpreter had understood my question or whether there was a mistranslation along the way, I have no way of knowing but I left with a frown on my face, none the wiser.

At lunch we were presented with a great quantity of sticky Japanese rice and a sort of overcooked seaweed, not unpleasant but pretty austere. Although we ate as much as we could there was a lot, particularly of the rice, left over which The Rock did his best to consume as presumably he didn't approve of waste or, maybe, he just liked rice! I heard much later that this same Master had allegedly developed a passion for cream cakes whilst presiding over a Sesshin in Switzerland. I hope this is not malicious gossip because, if so, I have done him a disservice.

One evening, shortly after returning from London, I was walking as I occasionally did, under the South Downs, along a picturesque meandering road to my nearest pub in the village of Fulking when a blue tit fell out of the sky into the bank of a nearby hedge. I leant down and picked it up. Its small beautiful but lifeless body was still warm, and I wondered where its life had gone and the strange thought occurred to me as to whether it now weighed any less. Did life have a weight? I laid the little exquisite body back in its resting place in the hedge. As I straightened up I glanced to my right where a whole field of sheep had turned their heads to look at me. Life, which had just been extinguished in one form, was now staring at me in another!

It was around this time that I asked myself the question 'what comes before thought?' Of course, the question was a thought! But clearly there had been life before thought. I realised I'd inadvertently set myself a Zen Koan, the best known of which is 'what is the sound of one hand clapping?' Unanswerable, at least intellectually. These and other questions engaged me along with my work and daily practice of concentration. And although I was feeling pretty good in myself, more easy-going and open, I slowly became somewhat disenchanted as I didn't feel I was understanding enough even though the deconstruction and unlearning process of the accumulated stuff, often called the 'ego', continued. A background hunger persisted. One evening, at dusk, I sat staring out the window of the tiny cottage in a sort of gentle despondency. An urgent question arose in my mind 'who am I, really?' As it arose, I suddenly saw that there wasn't a separate entity asking the question but that I was the question; so if I didn't know, who would answer!? The questioning mind stopped in its tracks having been rumbled, at least temporarily. No division, no separateness, peace and a sort of beauty of being. I was in touch with a quality of being 'before' thought. I don't think I'd ever slept as well as I did that night and yet the penny didn't quite drop.

Not long after, quite unexpectedly, I began a new relationship. My rented cottage was clearly too small, and a larger place was called for. After many unsuccessful forays, an estate agent directed us to a large Tudor farmhouse in 3 acres of land. Cheap at the time for reasons of a long, quarter mile bumpy access, a railway cutting not 50 yards away and restoration required. A Georgian extension had been tacked on to one end of the house. I suspect that it may have been built as payment by the Railways for allowing the cutting to pass through the owners' land. Maybe the end of the house was a barn extension that was in poor condition and the owners were only too pleased to have the money to replace it. In total there were 22 rooms! Cost £9,500. It was affordable even if it seemed a lot at the time. My father lent me the deposit, which I paid back after securing a mortgage. In those days you could borrow a bit more than the value of the house. This I needed to do, both to pay back my father but also to build a new pottery studio.

Plenty of hard work followed on the house to make it reasonably habitable. We both worked really hard but it gradually became obvious that we were not well suited, at least psychologically. This is not the forum to analyse the responses to the difficulties we both faced internally and externally. Emotionally, we were both immature but in very different ways.

For my part, I was naive, unprepared and ill-equipped to deal with the roller coaster of emotions that ensued. Over time I forgot everything I'd previously learnt, and my mistake was not to be honest about how I was feeling. I took on my parents' strategy of avoiding emotional stuff. The classic psychological 'transference' occurred, I blamed my partner for some of my difficulties and wanted her to change. I felt trapped and unable to handle the emotional turbulence. Mentally I was unnervingly troubled in what seemed to me to be an unresolvable and disturbing situation. I wanted to leave, but I'd built the studio for my work. Impasse. I remember going for a walk in a local wood and identifying with the young trees that had died from a lack of light. I was not in a good place. I was confused, exhausted, torn and broken.

2

An Unexpected Experience

We shall not cease from exploration
And the end of all our exploring
Will be to arrive where we started
And to know the place for the first time.
Little Gidding from the *Four Quartets* by T.S.Eliot.

On one ordinary day in the early summer of 1972 I came downstairs much troubled. For some months an inner turmoil had been exercising my attention. There was a lot of unresolved stuff going on exacerbated by emotional and financial difficulties, let alone being overtired by putting in too many hours of physically arduous work. As I approached the kitchen table my hand automatically stretched out to grab the packet of cigarettes off the sideboard. I flipped open the top expecting to extract a cigarette, but it was empty. This unexpected emptiness seemed to act as a trigger, for in the next instant there was a flash behind my eyes, and *everything* changed. I felt a need to go outside and without raising my eyes from the floor I walked slowly out the house and up the slight rise to the workshop. I knew something momentous had happened and quite why I kept my eyes to the ground until I reached the workshop, I'm not sure. I felt very physical, particularly conscious of the activity of walking, muscle movements etc. When inside the workshop I finally looked up and through the window I could see my favourite tree, the beautiful weeping larch.

What 'I' saw and felt is burnt into my memory. Everything was vibrantly but gently shimmering with the Light of Life. The trees, the flowers, the grass were all visibly pulsating, and it was clear that even the inanimate, the stones lining the path, were faintly glowing with a sort of 'potential' life. It was as if Life was not just a chance happening but an *inherent* quality of matter. There was present an immense silence and in this 'new' place, the acculturated self (that constructed edifice), wasn't. Consciousness was pure, direct and uncontaminated. A space that asked nothing but allowed everything. One was present noticing, witnessing. Small movements of thought, like eddies at the edge of a vast river, were swept away. They were irrelevant to this immensity, this Life Force. Out of this silence arose an intense affection for, and empathy with, all life. We are not separate. 'Life *is* one' suddenly made sense. No reason, no logic, beyond all that. The experience cannot be adequately conveyed. Language is a clumsy tool when something real happens. Poets might get close but it's still only descriptive. Nothing in my culture prepared me for this and I remember saying to a friend after the event, 'Who can one discuss this with?' 'Where is there help?'

Within the first few minutes of this extraordinary and unexpected experience I wrote down; consciousness – self = nonself consciousness. And simultaneously I smiled at the idea of death as the entity I had previously identified with, the 'me', that acculturated, conditioned self had, temporarily at least, died. What was left was the 'I', the *real* reality, the undivided, timeless, and incorruptible life force, sufficient unto itself, allowing everything, asking nothing and uncoloured by subjectivity. I was not so much in touch with the 'ground of being', I was it! And every other form of life, plant or animal was it too. Essentially, we are not separate from all life. I knew, without any doubt, that this understanding was where humanity was potentially headed, the implications of which, if achieved, would be, right now, almost inconceivable. It felt like I'd come home.

Bill Murray, a well-known Scottish mountaineer, had a powerful experience whilst in a prisoner of war camp during the Second World War. He expressed his experience of this deeper reality beautifully,

'The eternal world 'is'. Our material world is plainly real too: each inhere in the other: the finite within the infinite. The one embraces both.'
  From *Extraordinary Awakenings* by Steve Taylor.

The experience stayed with variable intensity for two to three days, at the end of which, and this is how I described it at the time, a shutter came down in my mind and I was back in 'normal' consciousness. But during those few days I noticed that in my interaction with others I responded rather than re-acted to situations. The responses were not conditioned, not conflicted but natural and unforced. What on earth was I, Joe Blogs, to make of this? It did occur to me at the time that if I'd been religious, a Christian or a Hindu for example, I might have interpreted the experience in the light of their teachings, but I didn't, I saw the experience in a purely existential way. Mysterious, yes, but very real and not to be barnacled by historical associations and therefore made unreal by ideation. Was I ready for this? Clearly not. Much later, a good friend of mine, who understands a lot more than I do, suggested that, like a cornered rat, my intense psychological suffering may have helped trigger the experience. At the time, I tried unsuccessfully to see the difference between this deeper reality and normal consciousness. The difference was experientially obvious but less amenable to analysis at least in this relatively short duration. I suspect one would need a few experiences to work things out and to stabilise the new perspective.

As I was remembering this experience and it's possible ramifications, I recalled the imagery of an analogy I'd first read about in Peter Russell's book 'The Awakening Earth' or the retitled American version 'The Global Brain Awakens', which applies well to the experience itself.

You are in the cinema watching a film. Images and dialogue play out the drama and you are hopefully absorbed in the story for a couple hours. Perhaps on the way home you discuss the merits of the film with your partner or friends, whether you liked it or not and why, or whether the production values, the photography, the story line were good or not so good, and so on. But does anyone talk about the screen? The screen allows the film to be seen whether good, bad or indifferent. Without it there would be no film. And the screen, the background, goes unnoticed like the life force, the ground of being, which asks nothing and allows everything.

Mind you, it is said that fish don't realise how important water is, the medium in which they swim until they are out of it and in the same way we don't really notice the importance of the gaseous air we breathe until we are denied it. Our conditioned lives are played out on an unnoticed background screen of unconditionality.

But notwithstanding the incredible privilege of having, albeit temporarily, touched the intense alive nowness of the very ground of our being, I found the effects, after returning to 'normal' consciousness, unsettling. The contrast between this expanded consciousness and normal consciousness seemed an unbridgeable chasm and yet one knew that that 'place' was home and that from such a place, if permanent, one could function with love and intelligence unencumbered by the narrowed perspective of 'self'. However, I was sufficiently disconcerted by this apparently unresolvable paradox, coupled with an equally unresolved emotional discordance within my relationship at the time, that I eventually headed for some sort of breakdown; so much so that for a two to three month period the idea of suicide became alarmingly attractive.

Fortunately I didn't go down that route but after an episode of catatonia, a sort of shutting down, not wishing to respond to questions or anything in particular, I decided something needed to be done, so I contacted my doctor. He put me in touch with a psychiatrist who, after a meeting with him, suggested I spent some time voluntarily in the local mental home to try and recover to the point where I could function relatively 'normally'.

Shortly after arriving at the imposing Victorian building, I was asked to change into my pyjamas and proceed to a designated room. On entering I was taken aback by the apparently Dickensian attitude to my plight. I was asked to sit in a chair in the middle of a room where 6 or 7 white-coated people, nurses or doctors I wasn't sure which, were present. I don't remember the questions I was asked or how I replied but at the time it seemed to me that this treatment, when one was at one's most vulnerable, was insensitive in the extreme. After interrogation I was escorted back to my assigned dormitory. Here I made my way to the corner of the room where I swayed back and forth from foot to foot. Much later I realised that I'd been physically acting out the English saying, 'not knowing which foot to stand on', a saying expressing distress and mental indecisiveness.

During this time, I wasn't allowed any visitors as 'they' wanted me to be away from outside influence. That was one of their better ideas. I was given various psychological tests and I talked to a more empathetic member of staff, one of the remaining skeleton staff members present, as it was my misfortune to be resident at the 'home' during the first ever psychiatrist's strike! One of the male nurses made it obvious that he didn't really want to be working as a nurse, as his prime objective was to train as a harpoonist and kill whales! I remember thinking at the time that he must be iller than I was.

After a month or so I was let out and to be honest I remember little of the next couple of months except that one day whilst attempting some kiln repairs, I found myself lying on the floor of my large oil kiln seemingly unable to move. Feeling like I was wearing a lead suit, I did finally force myself to stand and realised, perhaps belatedly that I could no longer stay in the situation I was in without risking being permanently put away, and I didn't want that. Necessarily, but sadly, I left behind my one year old son and two stepsons. So I drove to my parents' house and stayed with them for about a month. Clearly, they cared deeply and had been very worried about my situation but due to their upbringing were very uncomfortable with and therefore unwilling or seemingly unable to engage in mental/emotional stuff; it was not something 'one did'. It was behaviour that had been imbued in my psyche during my upbringing and wasn't helping me deal with the mental pain I was feeling at the time. Avoidance and dishonesty were at play.

The suicidal tendencies and the subsequent experience of breakdown and time spent in the mental home were at times terrifying, completely at odds with the other end of the mental spectrum where my unexpected 'oneness experience' was enlightening, reassuring and powerful. It has to be said that the rollercoaster of that and subsequent years left me with a certain psychological fragility strangely compensated by a much deeper appreciation of the interconnectedness of life and the urgent need for our species to address our often-destructive behaviour towards the extraordinary and wonderful expression of life in the natural world, which includes, of course, ourselves.

I needed to get away, so I called in an insurance policy realising enough cash to buy a green Ford Anglia van and leaving sufficient funds to last awhile. For several months I lived in the back of the van with my ever-faithful collie, Queenie. She found the experience more to her taste than I, less complex than a house, more like a kennel on wheels. Her enthusiasm kept my spirits up through a particularly difficult period in my life.

3

An Evolutionary Perspective

Let's take a brief look at the human story. We are a carbon-based life form living on a planet eight light minutes, 93,000,000 miles, from our life giving star, the Sun. Without her there would be no life. She is large enough to accommodate one million Earths and has been burning 600 million tons of hydrogen into helium every second for about 4 billion years. She is about halfway through her life. She is a third or fourth generation star formed from a vast and rich cloud of hydrogen gas and heavier atoms, on the outskirts of a spiral arm of a galaxy about 30,000 light years across, which we call the Milky Way. She is one of a hundred billion stars that make up our home galaxy and the Milky Way is just one of many billions of galaxies in the known universe.

Most scientists accept the present hypothesis that our universe began with the Big Bang, approximately 13.7 billion years ago. After the initial unimaginable incandescent heat and inflationary expansion, the first element to condense out of the conflagration was the hydrogen atom, then helium and perhaps a little lithium. And that's all the matter there was at that time. For the next hundred million years or so the universe was a dark place, until vast clouds of gas, composed of the first simple elements, started to slowly collapse under their own gravitational fields. The elements under compression gradually heated up until the temperature was sufficient for hydrogen atoms to fuse together in a thermonuclear fusion reaction requiring 15 million degrees Celsius to form helium, releasing enormous amounts of energy and light further heating up the gas and so on until an equilibrium was reached between the hot expanding gases outward pressure and the force of gravity's inward pressure. The first Stars were massive blue giants furiously burning through their fuel in as little as a million years. From helium, the nuclear fusion reactions continued to create carbon, nitrogen, sodium, oxygen, neon, magnesium and silicon releasing the energy necessary to keep up the outward pressure against gravity.

Supernovas are relatively rare astronomical phenomena. Stars which have solar masses between eight and fifteen times greater than our Sun are liable to go supernova when nuclear fusion tries to manufacture iron. This reaction uses more energy than it creates and therefore destabilises the stars equilibrium. Gravity takes over and the star dramatically implodes creating the most extraordinarily violent explosive power known. For a while it is brilliantly bright enough to outshine all the light from its own galaxy. The pressures and temperatures are such that all the other heavier-than-iron-elements are created and shot out into interstellar space at enormous speeds. The Hubble and now the James Webb space telescopes have photographed these beautiful nebulae, e.g. the Crab Nebula, remnants of these supernovas. The shock waves often disturb the nearby interstellar gases, creating density waves, such that new stars are born. The vast gas clouds thus become further seeded with more elements so the evolution of the next generation of stars is more complex than the last.

The gas cloud that collapsed to form our sun, being a third or fourth generation star, was element rich as was the few percent of material left over which formed our family of planets. Thus, Earth was well placed to contain all the elements necessary for complex life. All the different atoms in our bodies were thus created in stars, the first of which were only composed of 98% hydrogen and 2% helium. The universe evolved from this remarkable simplicity to the complexity we now see in our geology, our seas and all life forms. We are, as the saying goes, made of star stuff. So, our evolution is inextricably linked to the Big Bang, the beginning of time.

Early earth, which formed roughly 4.6 billion years ago, must have been an incessantly turbulent and violent place. Initially it would have been bombarded with stray rocks and asteroids, left over from planet formation, disrupting an uninviting atmosphere of hydrogen, carbon dioxide, methane, ammonia, hydrogen sulphide and water vapour. I imagine there would have been persistent high winds, torrential rain and powerful lightning strikes. Many active volcanoes would have been explosively punching out sulphurous gases and dust, initiating lava fields ending up in the steaming and restless seas. Scientific experiments have shown that amino acids, the building blocks of proteins and the earliest self-replicating molecule ribonucleic acid or RNA, are produced if an electric current (lightning strike) is passed through the above mentioned early atmosphere.

When and how life took form is difficult to establish and is therefore speculative. Many are of the opinion that very simple organisms, similar to present bacteria, may have evolved around hydrothermal vents under the sea or in the warm pools associated with geysers. Whatever was the case, life started its long evolutionary journey on Earth 3.5 billion years ago. It was another half a billion years before photosynthesis had evolved, a process taking CO_2 (carbon dioxide) and water and the energy of sunlight to synthesise sugars and producing, as a waste product, oxygen. This new waste product was the death nell for anaerobic bacteria but became the energy source for many new nascent animals. The waste product from oxygen-using cells was CO_2, the food source for plants. A nice feedback loop. Next, around 2.7 billion years ago, an extraordinary event took place, a cell or cells ingested bacteria, starting a symbiotic relationship that has survived to this day. Today we call that ingested bacteria, mitochondria, the energy powerhouse of all our cells.

But it was to be another 2 billion years before the simplest multicellular animals were able to collect food and maintain a stable internal environment. Although their bodies were still soft, bilateral symmetry was established with the ability to move away from danger as some creatures were learning how to ingest others as a food source. Slowly, in response to this danger, greater mobility and sensory capabilities for sight, hearing and smell, were developed. Competition between creatures was the starting gun that evolution needed and although there were several serious extinction events early on, creating precarious stop-start periods, evolution nevertheless, after the Cambrian extinction event 550 million years ago, exploded into all the main kingdoms we see today.

I think it's important to get a sense of the time scales involved here, in order to appreciate the perspective needed to view our extraordinary evolution. A thousand years repeated a thousand times is only one million years! Multiply one million years by another thousand times and you get 1 billion.

The emergence of the simple hydrogen atom, to the immense complexity of every living being on this precious planet, is simply amazing, bordering on the incredulous. Every living cell, for example, whether plant or animal, has three main structures. The nucleus holds all the genetic information in the form of chromosomes, long molecular helical strands, necessary to pass on species information to following generations. The mitochondria, small chemical factories creating the energy source for our muscles and general cell function, in the form of adenosine triphosphate or ATP. The protein manufacturing capacity resides in the third important structure called a ribosome. There are as many as a million in a single cell, producing complicated proteins at a rate of hundreds a second and if the manufacturing process is faulty, other chemicals are engaged to chop up and recycle the errant protein or proteins! And all this is happening in cells that the human eye cannot even see. This is a very simple description of the majestic, complex and beautiful evolutionary advances made in cellular development since life took form 3.5 billion years ago.

The seas were the first space that life conquered, and then as evolution, many many millions of years later, gathered pace, it moved onto the land with the early precursors of reptiles and arthropods. 370 million years ago the wood cell was invented, such that trees could invade the land— but only after algae and fungi had broken down the surface of rocks to create soil, aided by erosion. Life began to diversify across the land and continued to evolve different species to fill the niches and opportunities that availed themselves. Life was faced with multiple challenges but with the help of mutations and a natural selection of traits, prospered.

The next adventure for life was the vast and so far uninhabited opportunity of airspace. 330 million years ago the insects were the first to take flight, the flying reptiles followed 230 million years ago and later still, 150 million years ago, the birds.

Inner space or consciousness/awareness has been around since the first creatures became aware of their surroundings and the dangers lurking there. In its first incarnation, as perception and sensory awareness, it has served evolution well. It has been sufficient to carry evolution, over aeons of time, to an extraordinary level of sophistication.

Take the example of the peregrine falcon, which is the fastest animal on the planet, plummeting to catch prey at speeds of up to 200 miles an hour. In order to accomplish this, its nostrils have turned almost backwards so that they avoid the onrushing air, its eyes have evolved a transparent shield so it can still see at high speeds and, I love this bit, there are feathers which, at top speed, stick out of the otherwise streamlined body to minimise drag! Sharks have evolved cells which have the ability to pick up the faint electrical signals from hidden prey. Bats have developed sonar which allows them to form a picture of their surroundings. The sonic clicks are reflected off solid objects so that the bat can audibly 'see' its prey, usually moths, in the dark. The challenge to nature is/was to find solutions to problems which these physical and sensory adaptations beautifully display. Take any animal and there will be hundreds of physical and chemical adaptations internally and externally reflecting their specific needs relative to their environments and this is expressed in a wonderfully creative extravagance in the uniqueness of every being honed by nature. The mechanism which nature followed we now call Natural Selection, a process first understood by Charles Darwin largely through his study of the differently evolved beaks on the same species of finches adapting to different foods on separate Galapagos islands.

The next massive evolutionary leap in the human animal was the development of self-reflective consciousness. The ability to communicate through an exchange of understandable sounds, representing things in their lives, would have initiated a deeper comprehension of each other's needs and actions. Cetaceans were already employing sounds and clicks to organise hunting strategies, but their specialised adaptations coupled with their need to feed would necessarily inhibit any further conceptual development. Dolphins have been known to help or protect humans in danger showing a level of empathy and connection.

At some point a Chimpanzee had a eureka moment and realised one could use a hefty piece of wood or a stone to crack a particularly hard nut. Through watching and perception other chimps were able to learn but as yet their ability to communicate more complex ideas like the right size of stone and the best angle to attack the nut etc., hadn't yet evolved.

Humans released from the continuous need to feed had time to use this new ability to come up with ideas, initially expressed in simple words but later organised into an agreed language, further increasing sophisticated communication. Conception, not in the reproductive sense, was added to perception creating a new dimension, a new space in conscious understanding. In order for any language to function, it has to name things giving them a virtual existence in sound. This new ability allowed information to be passed between individuals initiating the beginnings of culture and cultural exchange. The very same advance had been made in early evolution when a library of genetic information was able to be passed from generation to generation through the agency of DNA (deoxyribonucleic acid). A different type of language but one which was creative and powerful enough to engender the extraordinary variety of life as we know it today.

This new ability of relaying information through sound meant that each generation could be creatively thoughtful when new challenges presented themselves. The cerebral cortex or frontal lobe consequently enlarged to accommodate the increased thinking capacity developed through the use of language and the birth of new ideas. When some bright spark realised you could take a chunk of flint, strike it with a stone or an antler to make flakes capable of stripping bark or flailing an animal's skin, then that knowledge could be passed on to his/her community. When building shelters in the jungle or making tents in deserts, each member of the community could add ideas as to the best way to accomplish such a task or make suggestions to improve a design.

Questions would have arisen around the mysteries of life and death, and beautiful creation stories evolved often interwoven with useful information and tribal wisdom, verbally passed, and no doubt elaborated on, from generation to generation. Later marks representing words or sounds were impressed into clay tablets and fired, and it is thought used by merchants for the purposes of notation and recording various goods for exchange. Later still the Egyptians used pictorial hieroglyphs as a language of military conquests and significant social and religious ideologies. The first known book, the Diamond Sutra, was printed in China in 868 A.D using wood blocks. In Europe the printing press was invented in the 15th century and quickly enabled knowledge to be further disseminated through the then educated classes.

Giving a name to a thing gives it an existence of its own, a representational virtual reality. Take a simple household object, a match box for example. When that word sound is picked up by our aural sense, we all agree, at least, in the English-speaking world, what it refers to and yet the matchbox's reality is not the word. This might seem an obvious observation but there are many less neutral words which might offend or be hurtful in some way. Maybe then it's not surprising that, depending how and with what each person's identity had been culturally cobbled together, that a sense of divisiveness or separateness could evolve.

We can all celebrate the wonderful developments that language has advanced in our societies over the millennia, and yet we have to acknowledge that this sense of separateness always contains the possibility of making us egotistically vulnerable to the criticism of some personally held ideas, beliefs or ideologies. Rather than being centred in our senses, our being and our vitality, we have too often become polarised to identify with divisive social, racial, military, political or religious ideas. This shift from experiential reality to the representational or virtual reality of naming created the initial phase of dissociation or separateness, giving ideas and concepts the power to divide.

In Nature, animals are constrained by their evolved specialities and by their genetically remembered instincts so that, without self-reflective consciousness, their choices are severely limited. Humans on the other hand, being perhaps the least specialised of all evolved animals, coupled with conscious choice, are not constrained. Their choices, their wants and desires, are only restrained by laws which recognise that some behaviours are inappropriate for a fairly functioning society. These laws reflect the fact that many of us, whether law abiding or not, are trying to get the best advantage for ourselves in a world which has put the ownership of money as a measure of status and, if one believes all the adverts, happiness!

Modern western culture, which has become the predominant model for prosperity and growth, has increased self-orientated behaviour as most of us are struggling to survive in a financially competitive and a not-particularly-caring society. This struggle to acquire sufficient finance to comfortably survive has taken the place of the struggle to find enough food, warmth and shelter, the main concerns of early man, and unfortunately are still the concerns of far too many today. Even though we may smile, it is still a dog-eat-dog situation for many. Unlike nature's process of Natural Selection, selection now is Unnatural in that one's status or financial position is often dependent upon an accident of birth. For those who make it to be comfortably off or rich even, most will understandably protect their position with various insurance policies, acquisitions and investments. But because of the acceptance within society of the normality of people to increase their wealth and their possessions as an admirable accomplishment, this behaviour is not considered selfish.

All we actually need, like early man, is enough food, warmth and shelter to healthily function, so why do we feel the need to fill our lives with more stuff, the latest watch, a new kitchen, upgrade to a new car and so on? This may be partly due to the practise of built in obsolescence in order to accommodate the latest model, keeping the factories thoughtlessly using up the earths limited resources. And partly due to the cultural conditioning of thinking that you'll be happier if you exercise retail therapy on a regular basis. The acquisitive 'me' is then constantly fed under the false promise of keeping one happy. The happiness is short lived and has to be regularly repeated. Social conditioning keeps us locked into these aspirational self-centred activities even if we have recently been made aware of the deleterious effects that such behaviour is having on the planet's biome and how, through the excessive use of fossil fuels for making and transporting such things, we are adversely affecting our climate.

It is salutary to realise that our planet has been looking after us for approximately 3.5 billion years. Optimum conditions for life have been kept relatively steady for much of that time through various positive and negative feedback loops brilliantly explained in James Lovelock's book 'Gaia'. In the same way, our bodies keep us in resilient stasis through the efficient functioning of our hearts, kidneys and all the other necessary internal organs, quietly, dispassionately and innocently looking after us whether we are an aggressive tyrant or someone who thinks of others before themselves.

So why do we not look after our home, our planet or our own bodies? Why do we not heed the warnings about stuffing ourselves with unhealthy processed food such that our bodies struggle with an excess of sugars and fats? Why do we continue to kill animals for the pleasure of eating them? Why do we not share our wealth with those less fortunate? Why, in the richer counties do we continue our profligate lifestyles consuming precious resources, not thinking of the impoverishment of future generations? Just in the last one hundred and fifty years the human animal has managed to progressively impoverish both terrestrial and atmospheric environments, negatively impacting both ourselves and the many other forms of life. And all these forms of life, plant and animal are innocent, except us. The allegory of Adam and Eve imaginatively describes our shift from innocence to knowledge. And our record of dealing with innocent plant or animal life has often shown us up to be unfeeling and selfish.

So what is it about our consciousness which blocks our ability to be sensitised to our bodies, to each other and to the planetary environment which has been our caring, evolutionary nursery over incredibly long aeons of time. How do we repay this majestic life-affirming generosity? With a thoughtless, care-less and ungrateful I'm-only-interested-in-me, me, me, culturally embedded attitude which necessitates the action of its co-conspirator, take, take, take.

When one considers that the world works perfectly outside the human mind, and that it is the content of our consciousness in the approximately 16 centimetres between our ears, that creates the problems we are presently facing, then one might reasonably deduce that nature's experiment of self-reflective consciousness has somehow back fired. However, self-reflectiveness is a very recent development and as yet we have not found a mature balance between the capacity of objective thinking located in the cerebral cortex and the largely subjective responses of the much older primal brain centre, part of which is called the hypothalamus.

My physiology lecturer at university declared that the functions of the hypothalamus could be abbreviated to the four f's, feeding, fighting, fleeing and sexual activity! The functions express the necessary adaptations for self-protection and for physical homeostasis in an ancient scary world coupled with the need to procreate. Fear and fighting, involving primary emotions such as anger and rage, evolved for physical self-preservation but if, as now, they are often connected to a personal or ideological protection of an idea or a belief, present only as a mentally held position, then one begins to see how aggression and violence towards one another comes about.

The present predominantly self-serving mindset is where our society finds itself right now, but if there is one thing that I can be certain of from my unexpected experience, it is that there is a much, much fuller and open-hearted potential waiting to be discovered within each one of us. Maybe then we can live up to the name Homo sapiens, meaning wise man, a name given to us by the Swedish father of modern biological classification, born in 1707, Carolus Linnaeus.

Footnote: The 'generative matrix' of the inflationary violence of the early universe, the ordered formation of the successive generation of stars and the forging of the awesome and wonderfully complex emergence of life's diversity is elegantly and imaginatively detailed in Brian Swimme and Thomas Berry's book, 'The Universe Story'.

In the meantime...

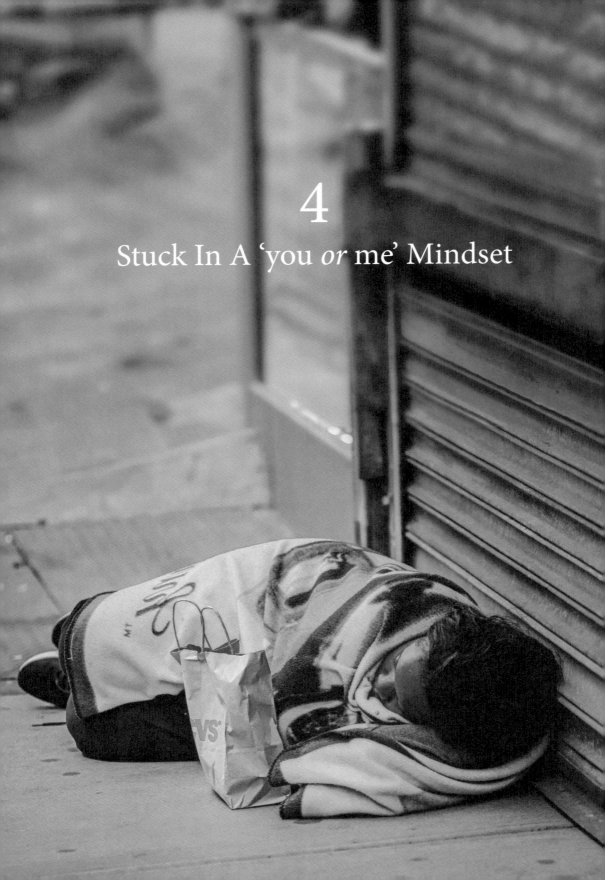

4

Stuck In A 'you *or* me' Mindset

'...to awaken the mind's attention from the lethargy of custom, and direct it to the loveliness and wonders of the world before us: an inexhaustible treasure, but which in consequence of the film of familiarity and selfish solicitude we have eyes, yet see not, ears that hear not and hearts that neither feel nor understand.'

Samuel Taylor Coleridge, 1772–1834, Poet, Historian and Cleric.

The operative word here is 'or'. It suggests separateness. I am separate from you. Physically it's true and certainly our psychological make up and our actions express this, personally, ideologically and politically. Apart from some rare exceptions, humanity has throughout the ages largely acted on this core belief. It is so normal it's accepted without challenge; it's simply assumed to be part of human existence. One of our worst expressions of this paradigm is thinking that we are superior to all other forms of life, plant or animal and that our needs and wants come first. Even amongst ourselves, this sense of separateness has often created religious, ethnic (racist) or political differences leading historically and presently to tribal rivalries or international wars. It has led to our exploitation and disrespect of the natural world, a world which is limited in its supply of raw materials, although from our unrelenting and excessively consumptive behaviour, you wouldn't think so. Essentially this psychology, this paradigm, this mindset can be expressed as a self-serving enterprise, me, me, me and/or take, take, take.

Whilst no blame should be attributed to the evolution of this present mindset, since it simply represents where we have got to so far, it is important to point out its failings, of which there are many. But it would be too depressing to concentrate on the inadequacies which such a mindset creates without upholding many of the wonderful qualities which we exhibit as a species in all areas of community life. Courage and kindness exist at the best end of this commonly self-serving mindset. And we have to acknowledge that societies have achieved extraordinary things within its limitations.

However, we seem stuck within a socially conditioned conformity where fear, twisted ambition, various forms of defensiveness and selfish agendas play out in the adult world, much of it learnt in childhood in reaction to the behaviour of others. There are many who are giving and caring and form the bedrock of 'normally functioning' society but even amongst these good people, when challenged, out from the psychological undergrowth, various forms of defensiveness can arise. It is this unexamined content of consciousness that creates the dysfunction within ourselves and society as a whole. It's still a jungle out there, it's still 'you *or* me', and what follows exemplifies the worst of this 'you *or* me' mindset, expressing the immense suffering we cause not only to nature and all it's wonderful forms of life but to ourselves and to one another.

'…we end up living inauthentically, playing roles and following conventions for the sake of others, disconnected from our deepest impulses…'
    Extraordinary Awakenings by Steve Taylor.

Those who hold power and control often consider themselves more important than the rest of us. It's endemic in our legal, political and financial institutions. Even if some people in high positions don't hold to this sense of superiority, they are happy to maintain the status quo. Our educational institutions encourage self-serving cleverness and competition in order for students to get what they want from society rather than contributing to what's really needed. And if you can afford it you can pay for a more privileged education to increase your chances of getting a higher paid job. The assumption being that private education is better and that you are more likely to land a better paid job if you are fortunate enough to come through this system. Certain occupations fall into this category, measured by their sociably accepted pay grades, politicians, doctors, lawyers, engineers, bankers, company directors, etc. But when you think about it, everyone contributes to the running of society whether working in undervalued occupations, like carers, and some manual jobs, for example. This is not to suggest that everyone should be paid equally but for the top 1% of earners to own approximately 40% of the nation's wealth is absurdly unbalanced leading to the politics of envy. These discrepancies and inequities are a natural consequence of the acceptance of a me-first, rather than another or community-first outlook.

Politicians seem powerless, or do not wish, to change this status quo, even though their primary remit is to look after the population. In my 80 years on this extraordinary planet, I've seen many political changes and heard many fine sounding promises, but the poor have continued to remain poor and living in often worse conditions and environments, whilst the rich continue to flourish despite the fancy words of 'change' from all political parties. Particularly in the West, but increasingly elsewhere, the rich seldom share their wealth with either the poor in their own country or with those less fortunate in the so called 'third world'. We seem content to watch poverty and suffering continue whilst we indulge ourselves with expensive cars, yachts, houses, luxury holidays, too many shoes and clothes, high end art, watches, jewellery, killing animals for pleasure, private jets and so on. And the me-centred outlook continues to surface as greed and corruption in our own institutions, often rightly exposed by the monthly British publication 'Private Eye'. The same can be said of the political and business classes in many of the emerging countries where the wealth created from rich resources doesn't address the poverty of their own people or provide them with adequate educational or medical facilities.

Charities try and fill the gap, but they too are subject to me-centred thinking, paying their CEOs and directors large salaries. I contacted a couple of well-known charities asking why it was necessary to pay such high salaries to their CEOs. One didn't answer, the other sent what felt like a standard letter saying that the salary was determined by the trustees, comparing the average pay to an equivalent position in industry. At the time the charity was asking for a regular donation of £2 a month. I worked out that it would take 5,800 years for one person to pay the CEOs annual salary of £140,000 at that rate! Or to put it another way, it would take 5,800 people paying £2 a month before any monies were put to practical use. And that's without including the directors' pay! The person giving the £2 would hope that their money would go directly to the advertised work of this charity but in reality, a significant amount of the money goes on salaries to the CEO and the eight directors amounting to a total of roughly £1,000,000 in this case. And then on flights, 4x4s, office rentals, computers etc. After such costs, the amount that is left that can be put to useful work, is less than 10% of the donations given.

Is it any wonder that things never seem to change? As soon as there is another famine, earthquake, flood or medical emergency, out come the heart wrenching images and pleas for help time and time again. Imagine how much more could be achieved if charities were really charitable and not run on a business model. I have met many who have, perhaps unsurprisingly, become sceptical as to the apparent ineffectiveness of their charitable donations. The 10% or less that does get through obviously does some good but surely donors should expect more efficient use of their money. And although there may be some much more effective charities, it's worth checking them out before deciding on a donation. Each charity is required to submit their annual accounts to the Charity Commission where such information can be found even if it's usually right at the end of their submissions. Charities are started to help the less fortunate in one way or another, but it seems that a lot of them end up disproportionally helping themselves.

EXPLOITING OTHERS

History records that the rich and powerful, which includes the military, have exploited the less fortunate. There are numerous examples of this abuse from the not-so-distant past to the present day. African slavery was officially abolished in 1807, but didn't come into full effect until the mid-eighteen hundreds due to plantation owners continuing the practice away from official legislation. But here in England, slavery of the indigenous white population particularly in the textile industries, was prevalent during the industrial revolution, including the use of children from the age of eight. Long working hours, 12 to 16 hours a day for six days a week with no compensation for injury or illness. The very low pay and poor living conditions forced some parents to have their children work beside them employed doing menial and often dangerous work amongst noisy and unprotected machinery. There was little or no political interest or intervention in this and other industries due to the prevailing Liberalism. Conditions were just as bad in coal mining for example where there were no rights or laws to protect the workers. Many entrepreneurs became immensely rich on the back of this suffering. Conditions started to improve in the 1850s when there was some political intervention in the form of workers' rights but not until workers in some factories withheld their labour until pay and conditions improved.

Recently in many parts of the Far East where, due to the cheapness of labour, western textile factories have relocated or subcontracted to local companies. In some of these, similar oppressive managerial practices have been employed in cramped working conditions just so that the richer westerners can buy cheap clothing. I can remember when a multi-storey factory in Bangladesh employing many young women caught fire and all tragically died because no fire exits had been provided. No one cared enough to provide them.

Today in Africa dangerous conditions exist in the unregulated cobalt mines. The miners, often quite young, get precious little for their efforts. The middle men and then the processing industries make the money so that we, in the richer countries can enjoy the batteries required in the present transitional economy.

Back in the eighteen hundreds, both in America and Europe white phosphorous was added to matches so that they would strike more easily. Soon it was observed that the women working in proximity to this new addition were developing necrosis of the jaw which presented itself as painful abscesses in their mouths leading to facial disfigurement and the loss of teeth. It was known as 'phossy' jaw. As early as 1852 Charles Dickens wrote about this condition in the publication 'Household Words'. It took another 18 years for its use to be banned but some unscrupulous factory owners continued its use for another 40 years. Can you imagine the suffering that that lack of concern created?

In early December 1984, on the outskirts of the Indian city of Bhopal, the Union Carbide factory suffered a massive explosion releasing 40 tons of methyl isocyanide gas into the air. This chemical was an intermediary in the production of the pesticide Sevin. Within hours 3,000 people had died and thousands more were condemned with cancers, miscarriages, stillbirths, congenital disabilities and drawn-out deaths. It was the worst chemical accident ever recorded but what is disgraceful about this tragedy is that no compensation was paid out until 5 years after the tragedy, delayed by various legal wrangles, and then much less than the Indian government had asked for. The factory has simply been left with insufficient chemical cleanup and the isolation of the surrounding area has been minimal. The company and its American directors/managers have never appeared in court, although some Indian employees were eventually convicted. No one has taken full responsibility for the suffering caused and both the Indian and American governments appear to have actively protected the new owners, Dow Chemicals, from any further legal repercussions. Many are still suffering to this day, 39 years later. This could only happen in a 'you *or* me' world where I am more important than you.

Today in southern Spain, in the region of Almeria, many of Europe's vegetables are grown under a plastic landscape covering 40,000 hectares. Workers, mostly North African migrants, work in temperatures of up to 50 C. Their living conditions are squalid and the wages poor. Returning to their own countries isn't an option for most as there is no work from whence they came or they would lose face for not finding the work which they left to find. And being paid so little they are unable to travel on, so they are effectively captive slaves. The conditions in which they live and the below minimum wages that they are paid contravene many of the rules of the ETI (the Ethical Trading Initiative). Many of the vegetables available in British supermarkets come from this area. The Spanish Ethical Trading Forum has increased awareness amongst suppliers, unions and grievance mechanisms but it seems that the vegetable producers have not been adequately challenged, so little or nothing has been done to end the wretchedness of the migrants. Is this because vegetable sales are an important aspect of the Spanish economy? There have been similar reports of migrant worker exploitation in the building sectors of the Middle East. In many businesses, philanthropy seems to be in short supply. The many continue to suffer at the expense of the few.

INEFFECTIVENESS

If you Google CITES, it states its aim as ' to ensure that no species of wild animal or plant becomes or remains subject to unsustainable exploitation because of international trade'. But unfortunately, it has proved to be pretty ineffective in carrying out its remit. This is a partly due to underfunding and partly to the inadequacy of its original wording. The convention covers international trade only, so that it fails to regulate the supply of wildlife products or to control consumer demand within the borders of any country (184 countries have signed up). And once an animal or plant is listed as endangered, its price and therefore the demand for it goes up. For example, Rhino horn jumped from $764 to $1,160 per kilo in the four years from 1980 to 1985.

The illegal trade in wildlife and wildlife products is worth $23 billion a year, the next in line behind arms, drugs and human trafficking. The World Bank estimates that just $260 million a year is allocated by governments to fight this illegal trade whilst $100 billion is made available to fight the illegal drug trade. In countries where digitisation is minimal, permitting relies on national paper-based systems which are easily forged. Export permits can claim that illegally harvested wild specimens are 'captive bred', for example.

It probably doesn't help that CITES is now responsible for 38,000 species, up from the original 700. It's estimated that 100 million plants and animals, both legally and illegally are trafficked each year for pets, traditional medicines and luxury foods. And the trade is estimated to have caused a decline of 60% in the abundance of species generally, and 80% in already endangered species. The most trafficked of these is the African scaly anteater, the pangolin, killed for its scales and used medicinally in China. Rhino horn and pangolin scales are made of the protein keratin, the same as our hair and nails. Rather than kill these wonderful animals, why not grind up human finger and nail clippings? Or, whilst humans still want to kill pigs and cows for food, why not use their trotters and hooves since they too are made of keratin? Not quite the same gravitas?

As already stated, CITES is massively underfunded and I'm sure the staff do their best from their Offices in Geneva, but whilst large financial gain is possible through poaching and trapping, policing the exploitation of our natural world is likely to continue to fall short and many of the species that have taken 3.5 billion years to evolve on this planet will be further diminished in number. There are moves afoot to improve the situation, particularly by the Australian NGO, Nature Needs More. At present it is simply a blueprint for saving and protecting wild species from a largely failed system. Time will tell.

If anyone has seen the difficult-to-watch Netflix film called Seaspiracy it would be hard to marry up the stated aims of the charity, the Marine Stewardship Council and the allegations against them in the film. The film, partly through the efforts of the environmentally campaigning ship, the Sea Shepherd, exposes the lack of Stewardship by the MSC and suggests that there is collusion between the big players, those massive trawlers which harvest vast numbers of fish at a time, and themselves. The word sustainable is used a lot by the MSC.

According to a paper by McGill University sustainability means 'meeting your needs without compromising the ability of future generations to meet theirs'. It applies to three main criteria: economic, environmental and social. Pretty vague, pretty wishy-washy! Guess what, the use of the term is unregulated, meaning that manufacturers and producers can use it if the product satisfies some, but not all of these criteria. Therefore, claims of sustainability cannot guarantee that a product has been manufactured in a way that does not exploit people or the planet or employ business practices that are unfair or unjust.

Take the example that back in 2004, in an effort to curb unsustainable growth, various stakeholders in the palm oil industry, (and I know that many people are concerned about palm oil and deforestation), the growers, the processors, the retailers, the manufacturers, the traders and the NGOs formed a non-profit organisation called the 'Roundtable on Sustainable Palm Oil' (RSPO). Today it is considered the gold standard of sustainable palm oil production. However, evidence provided by Greenpeace and Environment Agencies suggests otherwise. The investigations revealed corruption within the organisation itself, collusion with the stakeholders, continued proliferation of rainforest destruction and human worker exploitation amongst other lesser things. And yet palm oil marketed from such sources can still claim to be sustainable!

So, what do the MSC's claims of sustainability really mean? Back in the sixties and seventies the best fishing grounds in the world for cod were off the New England coast. Cod from there served the whole of Europe. Then in the 1980s the coastal fishermen realised that due to the massive offshore trawlers, the cod were disappearing. The US government were informed but took no action reassured by the trawler men that they were catching the fish in a sustainable way. Twelve years later, the fish were gone, and the industry collapsed ending the livelihoods of those associated with it. The seas are already grossly over fished, so what is being sustained? We, who should be stewards of this our beautiful home, need to *sustain* restraint until fish stocks are replenished and then leave the seas alone to flourish.

Last but not least, a topical subject, UK water companies and their continued mismanagement of our water and sewage systems. Whenever one questions why CEOs get paid so much out comes the inevitable platitude 'we must pay competitive packages to attract and retain the best people'. So, let's look at what the best people have been doing. I don't know what the terms and conditions were for the privatisation of our water utility companies back in 1989 but there was an unseemly rush, particularly from foreign investors to buy shares and since then 72 billion pounds have been paid out in dividends and the average pay for the CEOs in 2022 was £1.1 million a year. In the meantime, these best people have been dumping untreated sewage into our seas and rivers often, admitted OFWAT, illegally. This was first brought to our notice in 2016. Since then, millions of hours of raw sewage have been dumped into our rivers and seas. The dumping is only supposed to happen during heavy rainfall, an obligation that has been regularly ignored. One of OFWAT's remits is 'to make sure that the water companies properly carry out their functions'.

So, what have they done to enact their remit? And where is the Environment agency in all this? Are these regulatory bodies toothless, not given enough powers?

In 2021 the Lords' amendment 45 to the Environment Bill, which would have placed a legal duty on water companies to make improvements to their sewage systems and demonstrate progress in reducing discharges of untreated sewage, was put before parliament and, believe it or not, voted down! George Eustice, the Conservative environment minister at the time advised his members not to vote for the amendment essentially for four reasons a) the amendment came with no plan as how it could be delivered b) there was no impact assessment (surely that was already known, or does he mean the impact on the water companies?) c) it would cost too much! d) bills would have to rise too much (so not a vote winner then!). Now in 2024, raw untreated sewage is still being dumped through the storm overflow pipes into our rivers and seas, it keeps being reported and nothing keeps being done. So, the best people who have been paid huge salaries haven't managed to address the situation. They are clearly not intelligent enough to see the damage they are doing, or they simply don't care. So, in my book they are certainly not the best people. The profits, it seems, which should have been used to upgrade the essentially Victorian infrastructure over time have instead been largely redirected into the hands of greedy executives and shareholders. Ironically, these very water company executives and shareholders are made of 66% water!

These privatised utility companies are clearly not in the hands of the best men. Ben Elton, the English comedian and writer, recently fronted a TV programme on the privatisation of the train companies in the UK and he estimated that the cost to the tax-payer was £64 billion more than if they had been left in public ownership.

CREATING SUFFERING FOR ANIMALS

There are so many immature and unpalatable activities still supported by humans in many countries that I'll mention only a few of them. In England fox hunting was banned a few years ago but it is still sometimes illegally pursued. Mounted huntsmen and women with a pack of hounds chase a fox and if they catch it, the hounds rip the terrified animal apart. Oscar Wilde described it as 'The unspeakable chasing the uneatable'.

Many may be surprised that there are approximately 5,000 fur farms still operative in Europe, producing 60% of global mink and 70% of fox. Most of the rest is produced in the US, Russia and Poland, and some in the Far East. It's estimated that 50 million mink and 4 million foxes are annually slaughtered for their fur. Since living standards have improved in parts of Russia and China, demand has risen sharply despite the fact that excellent fake synthetic furs are now available. Glenda Jackson, the late fine British actress said 'No one needs a mink coat in this world…except minks'.

It should be remembered that many artists brushes are made from animal furs. I tried to research this once but came to the point that, apart from hair provided from established fur farms, fox and sable for example, the rest seemed to come from the shadowy world of unscrupulous traders. Sable, a member of the marten (related to the UK's pine marten) family of animals is farmed for its fur in the far east. Over half a million animals are killed annually for their particularly fine fur and sold at auction. It finds its way into fur coats and trims in high end clothing. Like furs, good synthetic brushes are available.

Some may remember back in 1984, David Bailey the photographer was asked by Greenpeace to produce a film about the fur trade. The uncomfortably realistic film depicts a catwalk model trailing a blood-stained fur coat with the slogan 'It takes up to 40 dumb animals to make a fur coat, but only one dumb animal to wear it.' It had a deservedly powerful impact at the time.

And how can anyone pay to see a bullfight in Spain (or watch it on television)? To watch an animal suffer and then to cheer at the skill of the matador, surely attests to a desensitised audience, untethered from feeling.

UDCA, Ursodeoxycholic acid was first synthesised from the bile of the genus Ursus (bears), hence its name. Medicinally it is used to help dissolve gallstones or cleanse the liver amongst other traditional medicine claims. In the Far East 10,000 mainly moon bears are still kept for their entire lives in tiny cages, mostly in China and some in Vietnam, in order to painfully harvest bile from a permanently open catheter or drip method. The bears used to be hunted and killed to obtain their gall bladders. Today cubs are taken from the wild and their parents often killed. There are charities rescuing bears from the farms or involved in persuading governments to halt the practise. Herbal and alternative synthesised products are now available. The fact that these barbaric farms still exist shames us all.

Live animal experimentation in medical research continues to be a contentious issue. There may be good reasons in exceptional cases for its use but there are many cons. One is that other animals used in experimentation, mostly mice, even if their DNA is 98% the same as ours, aren't physiologically the same. Their skin has very different absorbency rates to ours, for example, so that testing skin applications, creams etc. won't be accurate. The most powerful argument against is the case of the drug thalidomide, given to pregnant women roughly 50 years ago. Birth abnormalities started to appear, babies without properly developed arms and legs. The drug had been tested on a range of animals, including a close relative, the rhesus monkey, with no indications of problems. After the abnormalities surfaced, the same animals were retested again with repeated negative results. The pros and cons continue to be debated.

There has to be a balance between the improvements to human health and unnecessary experimentation.

In the US, the provision of mice in particular and their cages is big business. Students duplicate experiments over and over again in the many universities. How much suffering goes on I cannot say but much of the experimentation seems unnecessary and simply feeds an established industry. When I was at university studying medicine, I was surprised to find my physiology tutor was experimenting on a dog in a basement lab somewhere and then during a lecture a different teacher demonstrated that a decapitated cat still had certain reflexes!

These are just a few examples of our present seriously dysfunctional mindset and I have only just scratched the surface of our self-serving behaviours. I haven't even ventured into the problem of defensiveness which when extended from our minds to the outside world, necessitates the use of padlocks, various security systems protecting houses, factories, cars, computers, etc., and then on to the military where we require guns, tanks, drones, aircraft, missiles, armoured ships and now sophisticated computer systems to protect ourselves when irresolvable positions arise leading to personal grievances, legal battles and in the worst cases, wars.

Then there's child abuse, rape, human trafficking and forced prostitution, drug abuse, scamming, gender persecution, domestic violence, bribery and corruption, murder, knife crime, tax evasion, burglary, intimidation, fraud, female genital mutilation, organ harvesting, homelessness, habitat destruction, taking hostages, religious persecution, espionage, torture etc., etc., etc.

Clearly there is something profoundly dysfunctional with the way we behave and the suffering we continue to create amongst ourselves and the other life forms with whom we share this planet. We've somehow accepted that these aberrant behaviours are within 'normal' parameters, are part of human nature, and all we seem capable of doing at present is to legislate against such activities. We are not yet admitting that these behaviours have to do with the way we collectively think, the way we've been conditioned to behave.

The planet is having to adjust to our release of heat trapping chemicals, threatening ourselves and the delicate ecosystems that have evolved over long periods of time and many are already suffering from some alarming changes in weather patterns. Ironically many of the countries who have contributed the least to this problem, are suffering the most. And should we not be concerned that at a time when we know we should be minimising our use of energy, huge energy guzzling supermarket sized data centres are being hurriedly built to cope with the demand for streaming, gaming, photo storage and Artificial Intelligence etc.? Our excessive resource use cannot continue at the present rate. Are we thinking at all about our children and grandchildren or much further into the future? Roughly every 3 days, another million babies are born. They will all need food, water, and shelter as a minimum, but many will require fridges, phones, cars, furniture and so on, all of which require planetary resources. We have too successfully answered the call to 'go forth and multiply', such that we are creating deleterious effects everywhere. We are, in effect, 'shitting on our own doorstep' and still the politicians call for growth. It is clear that to them the maintenance of business sustainability is far more important than ecological sustainability. Apart from the Green Party and other environmentally concerned parties in the European Union, where are the farsighted mainstream politicians calling for the sort of sustainable economic policies, for a planet with limited resources, outlined in, for example, Tim Jackson's excellent book 'Prosperity Without Growth'?

'Anyone who believes that exponential growth can go on forever in a finite world is either a madman or an economist.'
Kenneth Boulding, 1910-1993, Economist and Author.

Our intelligence is unable to fully engage with the problems we face, as, being stuck in our present mindset, it is most often, certainly in business and politics, less so in the sciences, filtered through self-interest and assumes the lesser capacity of cleverness. Albert Einstein understood this well when he said in the oft quoted,

'The significant problems we face cannot be solved at the same level of thinking we were at when we created them.'

Intelligence, when allowed to function, dispassionately takes all relevant factors into account and then acts for the good of the whole. But we function within the spectrum of selfishness, from the extremes of criminal self-interest to relative unselfishness. It doesn't seem to occur to us that our actions are an expression of our consciousness and it's acculturated content. We are all swimming in a sea of various degrees of selfishness but because we are all in the same boat, as it were, we don't recognise it, it is so normal. Initially, perhaps, it's not that easy to see that our centuries old 'you *or* me' mindset is essentially selfish and that there are millions of individuals out there all fighting in our society's Darwinian cut-throat survival-of-the-fittest mode.

And as we presently measure success in terms of money and property, we have seen that those who survive best aren't really helping those less fortunate or being ecologically responsible in their business or financial activities. And the rest of us are collectively similarly limited by the socially encouraged self-serving me, me, me, attitudes. Our selfishness is selling us short. But is there an alternative? Is there a potential within each of us to further evolve into a selfless field of consciousness where me-centredness plays an insignificant role and where intelligence can finally find its proper place, it's home?

ADVERSARIAL POLITICS

Occasionally here in England I turn on Prime Minister's question time. I'm always hoping to see mature objective answers to well thought out questions. Instead, there is a pathetic puerile, often antagonistic exchange of entrenched positions. Jeering like schoolchildren, snubbing each other with their thumbs on their noses, wagging their fingers. How is this constructive? The energy that is wasted in such exchanges and the subsequent positionality of party politics which may have worked in western democracy for several hundred years but now seems completely inadequate for today's very serious concerns. Each party, once in power, wants to change things to fit their philosophy. They fiddle with the economy, transport, health, and so on, more from political expediency rather than trying to objectively get to a point over time, and they've had plenty of time, where the systems work really well and efficiently.

I'm sure, in government, that there are committees where cross-party objective appraisals are carried out and sensible decisions arrived at. But maybe it's too much to expect that politicians might be chosen for their objectivity and wisdom and, personal agendas aside, could make decisions for the good of the whole, decisions which would last and cease to be as short term and financially wasteful as they are at present. If, from the perspective of our present 'you *or* me' mindset, this sounds idealistic, nevertheless it remains an achievable possibility if we are able to shift to a more mature level of consciousness.

WARS

Wikipedia distinguishes between major wars, wars, minor conflicts and skirmishes. The list is long, with Africa suffering the most but Asia and South America not far behind. Throughout our history there have existed ideological, political and religious differences. Wars only exist as a manifestation of the intransigence in our minds. Intractable positions lead inevitably to skirmishes or full-scale wars, whether intentionally started or not. Retaliatory retribution for historical grievances flare up periodically in parts of the world like right now in Israel and Palestine. Power hungry and expansionist individuals like Putin, for example, are creating appalling destruction in Ukraine, unconcerned it seems with the suffering he's causing. And religious fanatics, as in Iran, are using violent edicts to create unnecessary suffering for their own people. The unexamined content of our consciousness is at the heart of this havoc. Can we grow up?

So, what is it about our consciousness that creates this ghastly and enduring suffering? Before thought, none of these conflagrations could have happened. Once we became self-aware and acquired the ability to think and manipulate words, concepts and beliefs, divisions started to occur. We shifted our centre of reality from perception and being to conception, having and becoming. It is our thoughts and emotions, that is, the content of our minds, which separates us, whereas our primary and essential reality is one of being and an undivided field of consciousness. If centred in being, differences would still exist but discussions, when necessary, wouldn't be elevated to violence, but would find resolution through in depth conversation and compromise.

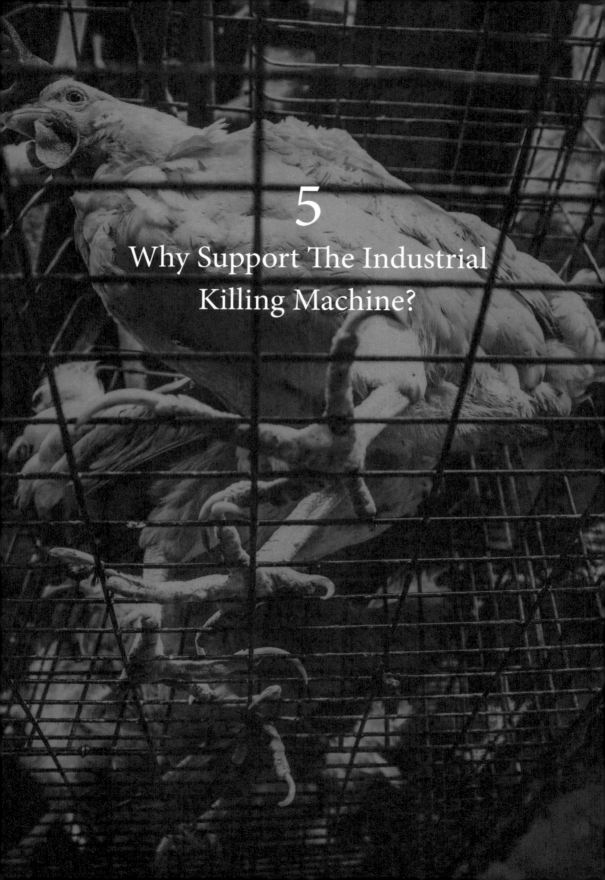

5

Why Support The Industrial
Killing Machine?

'Nothing will benefit human health and increase chances of survival of life on Earth as much as the evolution to a vegetarian diet.'

Albert Einstein, 1879-1955.

Unless we allow ourselves to question, we don't really become conscious of our conditioning. Every culture has their own unthinking acceptance of some traditional way of thinking whether religious, political or personal. The Pavlovian repetition of opinions is commonplace. Conformity is pretty much the norm even amongst those who consider themselves freethinkers. To have an opinion is easy enough but to have a fully informed opinion requires work to find out the relevant objective facts. I say objective since there is much that is out there that is sensationalised and emotionally charged. Just to illustrate our biased conditioning in this country, a local village recently had a hog roast with music and dance in the evening after an afternoon fete. Presumably a committee had collectively agreed to this, and I wondered whether there would have been such willing agreement if a dog roast had been suggested.

The killing of animals for food needs to be re-examined. There are those who consider vegetarians as unmacho wimps; there are those who eat meat but claim they would never harm or kill an animal, blindly refusing to take personal responsibility for the killing; there are those who only eat organically produced meat, conveniently forgetting, it would seem, the journey to, and the associated stress of the slaughterhouse; and there are many who've never thought about it at all. So here I've described some straightforward facts about how the majority of food animals are kept and destroyed in a country where we apparently pride ourselves as animal lovers!

In Britain almost all turkeys and broiler chickens are intensively reared in large industrial-sized sheds. As they grow and develop, aided by selective breeding, overcrowding is the norm. In these excessively cramped conditions, the birds have no option but to stand in their own faeces. Chemical burns to the feet and legs (hock burns, where the ammonia from the waste has burned through the skin of the leg) are commonplace. Turkeys in particular, although it happens to the broiler chickens too, suffer both broken legs and heart attacks due to the speed of weight increase in these young birds. Because of the completely unnatural stocking densities the birds peck at one another indicating the stress they experience living in such close proximity. A common solution to this is to trim the beaks of turkeys and layer hens. Broiler chickens reach the optimum weight of 2.5 kilograms at five weeks and are slaughtered shortly afterwards. Turkeys are killed anywhere between 12 and 25 weeks depending on the weight required. These hothouse conditions enable farmers to produce cheaper meat, encouraging more consumption.

Intensively farmed pigs are not treated any better. Having nothing to do in the overcrowded, usually cement floored sheds, the young and curious piglets bite at each other's ears and tails. To discourage this behaviour their teeth are usually clipped, and their tails snipped off without anaesthetic. Their mothers, the sows, are restrained in a metal cage not even large enough to turn around in, but just big enough to allow her young piglets to reach her teats but not big enough for her to interact with them. As soon as they are weaned, the young pigs are removed to be fattened up, the sow is re-impregnated and the whole unnatural cycle is repeated until the viability of the sow ends and she is sent to slaughter. Depending on the type of meat required, the young pigs are destroyed at between five and six months old.

The romantic idea of dairy cows living a contented life grazing England's green and pleasant land is far from the truth. The demand for high yields and cheap milk has created an industry of considerable suffering for most dairy cattle. Whilst pregnant she produces around 22 litres of milk a day whilst at the same time trying to feed herself and her growing embryonic calf. Carrying such a weight puts an extra strain on her haunches and can often create leg and foot problems due to her widened gait. Mastitis, a painful infection of the udders is dormant in about 20% of herds and active in a much smaller percentage, so pus from the infection enters the milk. Milk with a somatic 'pus' cell count of more than 400,000 cells per millilitre is deemed unfit for human consumption. In the US the legal limit is 750,000. It is perfectly safe to drink such milk due to pasteurisation, it's just that the idea of its presence is less palatable. The cow's natural life span of 20 years is reduced to 5 or 6 years when she is sent to slaughter due to exhaustion and a reduced milk yield. Her daughters will follow her difficult life whilst her sons are sent to slaughter or sold on to produce cheap meat.

Intensively reared egg producing chickens have to spend up to two years in tiny wire cages. No foraging, no exercising their natural curiosity and hardly enough space to preen. Painful beak trimming is practiced to curb the damage from aggressive behaviour induced by the unnatural conditions in which they are kept. When the young hatchlings are sexed, most of the males are killed either by being gassed or in some cases, macerated.

And then there's fish. The World Watch Institute were calling for an end to overfishing back in the nineties due to diminishing stocks and to give the oceans time to recover. The fishing industry with their huge factory ships took little notice and continued to operate at greater depths catching lesser-known species. Fish are one of the last wild animals that are extensively hunted across the world. Each year approximately 80 to 100 million tonnes are caught and killed. Those caught in trawl nets are often crushed to death under the weight of the catch. Fish that are still alive by the time they reach the decks of the fishing boat either suffocate or are disembowelled with a gutting knife. It is not only the fish that suffer. The fishing nets catch dolphins, porpoises, sharks, turtles, diving sea birds, sea stars, crabs, shellfish and many other creatures- as well as species of fish which are unwanted.

On the 15th of September, 2021, I woke up to the distressing news that the Faroe Islanders had slaughtered a pod of 1,426 white finned dolphins. Usually the pods are 300 to 500 strong but this super pod was herded into the shallows of a beach on the Isle of Eysturoy. The method of killing was to stab the dolphins in the neck and then to cut the carotid artery and spinal cord. Because there were far too few slaughterers in the sea, many of the dolphins suffered prolonged deaths. Up to 50 yards out, the sea was red with blood and many islanders came out to watch the morbid spectacle. The Faroe Government said that the kills of dolphins and long finned pilot whales provide an important food source for the islanders. Such killing had been a traditional activity since the Vikings settled in the cluster of 18 islands in approximately 800 AD.

It was clear that many were upset on hearing the news. Cetaceans are considered to be a very intelligent group of animals but so are other animals farmed for food, pigs for example and, in Korea, dogs. But what is the difference between this slaughter and the mass slaughter that goes on behind closed doors in the UK's abattoirs except that the killing of the dolphins was in plain sight. So, are there double standards here? Who, amongst meat-eaters, are upset at the 137,000 animals killed every hour here in the UK? Surely these days, except in exceptional circumstances like survival in life threatening situations, none of these practices are appropriate or necessary.

This is only a brief outline of how we treat our fellow creatures. I have not covered the factory farming of ducks, mutton or beef production, the forced feeding of geese to create foie gras (banned in this country but imports allowed), salmon and shrimp farming, the catching of sharks, removing their fins with a sharp knife and releasing them back into the ocean to die, just for the delicacy of shark fin soup. Then there's ostrich and deer farming, pheasant shooting, whaling, and live animal 'wet' markets, common in many parts of the world, notably China, Southeast and Southern Asia where any creature may be fair game, from snakes to civet cats. And the only time the industry seems to really care about its 'products' is in the presentation of attractive packaging on supermarket shelves.

Here, in Britain and no doubt elsewhere, there are farmers who are properly concerned with their animals' welfare. There are fewer of them now as various pressures, including cost increases are not making it any easier to continue a viable business. But regardless of the method of rearing that a farm animal has experienced it still has the horrendous ordeal of transportation to and death at the slaughterhouse. And these slaughterhouses are hidden from view, out of sight and hopefully as far as the industry is concerned, out of mind. To make matters worse, in the drive to keep the price of meat down, the animal food processors are developing faster ways of killing and processing carcasses, creating even more unnecessary suffering. There are now machines that are approaching the capability of mechanically killing and eviscerating 15,000 chickens an hour. In this mindless process, faecal matter can spill onto part of the chicken that people like to eat i.e. the skin, increasing the possibility of bacterial infection.

'You have just dined, and however scrupulously the slaughterhouse is concealed in the graceful distance of miles, there is complicity.'
   Ralph Waldo Emerson, 1803-1882, Essayist and philosopher.

The recent pandemic should give us pause to rethink how we treat 'food' animals whether in the live 'wet' markets in the Far East or in the uncivilised conditions of factory farms mostly in the western world. In both cases the transference of viruses from one species to another (zoonosis) is increasingly likely. High animal densities, low genetic diversity and the overuse of antibiotics greatly assists virus mutation seriously risking further zoonotic outbreaks.

A while back Viva! exposed the suffering of horses being transported the long distance from Poland to Italy where it is more acceptable to eat horse meat. The lack of care during the trip often resulted in dehydration and broken limbs were not uncommon. Perhaps the worst case I came across was one reported from America. Pigs were being transported a long distance and on arrival at the abattoir a few animals were found to be frozen to the lorry's metal stanchions. The solution- chainsaw them loose whilst still alive! It is hard to imagine the insensitivity and lack of feeling required to do that. But, given the brutality of the job, are not those whom we expect to do this for us, themselves brutalised? How else could they do it? If this and other abuses sadden and disturb you, then don't create the need for them.

'Even if conditions for animal welfare are improved and the rearing which takes place behind the closed doors of factory farms is banned, a fundamental issue still remains: is it ethical to kill animals because people enjoy eating them? We should quietly reflect on whether meat-eating can be part of a genuinely caring society.'
  Actions Speak Louder Than Words by Iain Scott.

In the U.K, let alone the rest of the world, 1.2 billion land animals are annually slaughtered for meat. 1 billion fish and 4.4 billion shellfish are caught and consumed. If my maths is correct this equates to the slaughter of 100 million land animals a month, 23 million a week, over 3 million a day and the staggering figure of approximately 137,000 slaughtered every hour of every day! That's approaching twice the capacity of Manchester United's football stadium every hour. And that's just the U.K.

Recent IPCC (Intergovernmental Panel for Climate Change) reports have drawn attention to the extensive environmental damage created by the meat industry. Apart from the degradation and deforestation of the tropical rain forests by cattle ranchers, particularly in the Amazon, the industry's contribution to global warming is highlighted. Strong advice to cut down on meat consumption is quickly and conveniently forgotten. And that's without mentioning the alarming amount of water used in beef production, approximately 15,000 litres per kilo! Instead, news outlets concentrate on air travel and other forms of transport. Depending on which reports you read the carbon dioxide (CO_2) emissions from these two sectors is fairly equivalent, between 15 and 18%. Additional to this, the rearing of cattle for meat is responsible for the following global warming emissions; 37% of methane (23 times more polluting than CO_2); and 63% of nitrous oxide (295 times more polluting). We are told to limit flying but not our meat consumption. Is this indicative of the power of the meat lobby?

What's more important to you, the taste of the flesh of a slaughtered animal or its life? Given conscious choice and without the justification of need, the killing becomes, let's face it, a thoughtless and brutal self-indulgence so deep rooted in our culture that it is seldom addressed. It is considered so normal that few give it a second thought. I am deeply convinced that our cultural myopia towards viewing other life forms as simply fodder or clothing or experimental tools or sport is fundamentally blocking our ability to see life as interconnected, as part of ourselves. If we could see it, we could then engender the principle of coexistence in deep respect of what other species, both plant and animal, need and want. If we can make this paradigm shift, I'm sure we will look back in amazement at our sickening arrogance and insensitivity with a profound sense of shame.

'I have from an early age abjured (avoided) the use of meat and the time will come when men such as I will look upon the murder of animals as they now look upon the murder of men.'
Leonardo da Vinci, 1452-1519.

Historically, going back probably to the invention of fire, man has eaten meat and utilised skins for clothes, bone for needles and antlers for flint knapping etc. We were opportunists and in order to survive we needed such things. Today it is still appropriate for many northern tribes, e.g. the Caribou herders of the Russian and Mongolian Steppes, to be sustained by 'their' animals. After all there is not much else on the menu and their skins provide material for their tents, footwear and clothing. So, it is not a matter of what's right or wrong but what's appropriate in a given set of circumstances. Not in the cold North or South but in temperate climes, we need to ask ourselves if subjecting animals, as we have seen, to the appalling conditions of factory farming and the journeys to the killing houses or abattoirs, is the appropriate ethical behaviour of a supposed-to-be-civilised human?

As we spread across the world out of Africa, we no doubt faced many dietary challenges. Being naturally resourceful we became culturally omnivorous. Physiologically, though, we have remained frugivorous, evolved and adapted to receive all our dietary needs, proteins, fats and carbohydrates from a diet of seeds, nuts, fruit and root vegetables, not meat. Animals who eat meat (obligate carnivores) have large incisors for tearing at flesh and short guts to speed the evacuation of toxic waste products. We, on the other hand have long guts and teeth designed for biting and chewing.

Some may argue that nature is 'red in tooth and claw'. And it is true that without the predator/prey relationship no significant evolution would have taken place but this doesn't justify the continuance of meat eating at a time when we are no longer in survival mode and can conveniently buy food from stores ready packaged. As it happens our species has evolved the capacity of self-reflection and choice. If we continue to choose to kill for pleasure, so be it. But we have the capacity to be bigger than that, to be more thoughtful and caring, to be more humane.

It is interesting to note that many of the Greek and Roman philosophers were fiercely vegetarian. Here's a selection of their thoughts.

'Alas, what wickedness to swallow flesh into our own flesh, to fatten our greedy bodies by cramming in other bodies, by having one living creature fed by the death of another.'
   Pythagoras, from the sixth century BC.

'What with our hooks, snares, nets and dogs, we are at war with all living creatures and nothing comes amiss but that which is either too cheap or too common; and all this to gratify a fantastical palate.'
   Seneca 5 BC-65 AD.

'I, for my part, wonder of what sort of feeling, mind or reason, that man was first possessed to pollute his mouth with gore and to allow his lips to touch the flesh of a murdered being; who was to spread his table with the mangled forms of dead bodies and claimed as daily food and dainty dishes what but now were beings endowed with movement, perception and with voice.'
   Plutarch, 46-120 AD.

Powerful feelings expressed up to 2,600 years ago. But still, after all this time, we destroy worldwide, around 79 billion animals a year, roughly ten times the number of people on the planet. I repeat 79 billion. Civilised? Think again. The vast amount of land used to grow food for them would be far better used to grow food for us or better still given back to nature or a mixture of the two. So, the question remains 'why do we persist in eating the dead flesh of animals?' And, in consequence, why do we allow the continuance of the industrial killing machine? It's alarmingly sad, but simple, because people like the taste! And this taste sensation is encouraged through a burgeoning array of cookbooks, magazine articles, barbecue recipes, fast food outlets and the numerous TV cookery programmes fronted by well-known celebrity chefs where meat is 'taste'fully presented avoiding the pain and suffering involved. But none of them, offer the information you need to make an informed choice. Do we need to ask why? Linda McCartney understood this when she said, 'If slaughterhouses had glass walls, everyone would be vegetarian.'

My own shift in understanding, my own change of heart happened unexpectedly one morning. When I was about 24, at my first pottery, it was my habit to let my adventurous border collie out first thing and, if the horse was present in the neighbouring field, she would shoot off and the two would, with great enthusiasm, chase each other about for a while. Coffee in hand, I would, if the day was fine, stroll out and lean on the fence to be with them. When they decided that enough exercise had been employed, both would trot over, bright-eyed and breathless, to see me. It became a regular occurrence, something enjoyable for all of us. On one particular morning the horse came over for her customary head stroke and nuzzle and I, for some unknown reason, looked intensely into her eyes. I was in for a shock. In an instant it became crystal clear to me that the horse's life and my own were one and the same. Yes, she had a different shape, different mental processes, a different metabolism even but the experience was that the ground of our being, our life force, was the same. A thought spontaneously arose in my mind 'I don't want any animal to suffer or die on my account'. It was that simple, I had, in no time at all, with no consideration become a committed vegetarian. Little did I know at the time how this intuition would eventually deepen.

To go vegetarian or vegan is usually a considered, conscious choice to minimise the unnecessary suffering and death for those animals presently destined to be eaten. Ending our selfish meat-eating habit will have positive political and environmental ramifications. It is not always easy to make the shift to a no meat diet, especially if one is surrounded by derisory and unsupportive attitudes. I once met a Scottish woman who, at the age of eight, had decided to become a vegetarian. She was stoically unpersuaded by parental pressure to revert. Her decision was ethical; it was civilised;

it was compassionate and from the evidence of most nutritional studies, healthier.

Even if we can mature and become a more genuinely thoughtful and compassionate society, some animal products will still be necessary. Our pets, dogs and cats in particular, are obligate carnivores and need meat as a regular part of their diet. We need grazing animals as many wildflower species have evolved in the grasslands grazed by horses, cows, deer and sheep. Wool and leather are important materials for warm clothing, saddlery and even cricket balls! But the obscene amount of killing that goes on at present has created a massive surplus of animal skin and to cope with this excess, industries have mushroomed for the manufacture of car seats, sofas, jackets, shoes, gloves and handbags etc.

And whilst human populations remain unsustainably high, the culling of certain species such as deer and boar, for example, will be necessary to maintain the forests and limited land that they are given to occupy. If we are to maintain our zoos, feeding the many carnivore species, lions, tigers, leopards, panthers, hyenas and raptors etc, a regular supply of meat will be required. So, killing cannot be avoided, but it'll no longer be killing for pleasure. Animals, mainly cows and sheep, who provide meat, milk, leather and wool would be kept in conditions as close as possible to their natural environment and only humanely killed towards the end of their usual lifespan (approximately 20 years for a cow).

I'm going to finish this chapter with part of an article I wrote back in 1994 with the artist community in mind, called 'A Deeper Connection'.

'While I write this the swallows are amassing and fattening up for their annual flight to Africa. The dragonflies are active in laying their last eggs in the pond. The squirrels are conscientiously burying the hazelnuts amongst the flowers and the crane flies are punching their ovipositors into the lawn and the last flush of autumn flowers are dignifying the perennial beds. Isn't

it extraordinary? Doesn't it raise joy in our hearts? Doesn't it confound our minds how all this came to be? So why can't we extend this wonder outwards to all other species? If we are so rightly concerned with the expression or re-expression of beauty and vitality in our culture, why do we condone the callous, life-denying ugliness of our killing houses, however well disguised their products, whether on our backs or on our feet or on our plates? As an animal, do we not consider our own lives as precious, so why not others? The right to life in all its manifest forms is unfortunately a context far removed from our present speciesism.'

From *An Autobiography of Sorts.*

6
Why Belief?

'You can believe anything you want to believe in.'

Demosthenes, 4th century BC, statesman and orator.

Belief in someone or something means you don't know. If you knew you wouldn't need to believe. I remember, about 30 years ago, listening to an interview with Richard Feynman, the American physicist and mathematician in which he was asked about belief. Effectively he said, belief closes you down, you can no longer learn anything new, at least not in that area. So mentally, he said, the best place to be is 'not to know' so that you are open to the new. Enquiry continues to be possible. Interestingly the word 'innocence' means 'not to know'.

Having said that, one can easily imagine how beliefs arose. In the lives of early humans, mystery was everywhere. Why did the sun rise in the morning, cross the sky and disappear later in the day? Why did the sky create thunderous noise and flash with light? Why did disease arise? Why did people get old and die? Where did they go? Was there an afterlife? And so on. It's unsurprising that explanations were sought for these and other mysteries presented to the emerging consciousness of man. Lawrence Van de Post mentions, in one of his books, the delightful bushmen explanation for the stars in the night sky – a blanket with holes in it!

Any animal or plant had its own spirit. Even inanimate mountains and waterfalls had their own spirits. If unexplained diseases, stillbirths, early deaths and other misfortunes occurred, it was in many cases thought that the spirits were unhappy. And to appease them various redeeming, sacrificial and ritual practices evolved.

At some point, the work of taking care of the 'spiritual' lives of the tribe, was delegated to one person. As societies grew in size and complexity, spiritual guides or shaman became increasingly powerful to the point of being influential in the decisions of the political classes. In the 3,000 years of the extraordinary Egyptian Culture the spirits had evolved into approximately 1400 deities who were responsible for all facets of everyday life. Their wonderful temples and pyramids attest to the power of their beliefs and/or the needs and fears of the reigning Pharaohs. Only very strong beliefs and fears would be capable of galvanising such a large workforce into expressing in stone such monumental extravagance and beauty. Worship of and sometimes sacrifices to these imagined gods was commonplace in specific religious ceremonies. Later many other cultures created extraordinary religious buildings, the Mayans in Central America, the Buddhist temples at Angkor Wat in Cambodia, the Hindu temples in India, the Stupas and Pagodas of the far east, to mention just a few. Nearer home, in Europe, Cathedral building was at its height in the 11th to 13th centuries. Reading about this fertile building period, I was made aware that the many design improvements and size increases were due more to the ambitions of the priesthood in trying to outdo their 'competitors' than for need. Bishops at this time were all powerful, rich and often corrupt.

Hinduism has 6 major gods and 33 subsidiaries; Buddhism, being a philosophy, has no gods but perhaps due to the fertile imagination of the Indian culture, has many helpful spirits; The Mayans had between 166 and 250 gods and goddesses; The Inca, 3 main gods and 48 subsidiaries. The major world religions are Buddhism, Christianity, Hinduism, Islam, Confucianism (perhaps more of a social philosophy), Judaism, Baha'i, Jainism, Shinto, Zen, Sikhism, Rastafarianism and Zoroastrianism. And I'm sure there are many other minor beliefs which I'm unaware of. The plethora of beliefs, superstitions and imaginary gods have become progressively more complex and embedded over time. Many have achieved mythological status. Different interpretations of the perceived truth are rife extending from the sophisticated Sanskrit commentaries on ancient

Hindu texts to the risible rants of the tub-thumping TV evangelists who apparently know what God wants for us!

In the Christian world the structures of belief were hard won over many centuries. Anyone who has studied the Councils of Nicaea and subsequent councils, will realise that foundational Christian doctrines were debated over many centuries until they became cemented in theological stone. Even at the first meeting in 325 AD, splits and factions were already evident. These meetings were an attempt by church leaders to reach a consensus on orthodoxy, in the hope of developing a more unified church. The first meeting settled the debate in favour of those who argued that Jesus was the son of God. The second meeting in 381 AD established, amongst other things, the divinity of the Holy Spirit and in the third meeting in 431 AD the theological nature of the Virgin Mary was discussed. Those who wanted to call Mary 'the Christ-bearer', the Nestorians, were thrown out of the main church in favour of those who wanted to call her 'the God-bearer'. The last meeting was convened in 787 AD. All this theological and liturgical scaffolding took a long time to erect, and the debates continue to this day. It is all head stuff serving what purpose?

Many millions of people find belief to be personally helpful and gives them strength in conducting their daily lives but perhaps more important than that is the deeply comforting feeling of trusting some 'higher power' in an unpredictable, often harsh and painful world. And knowing that many others share that same faith is a socially cohesive solace. Whether it's true or not seems irrelevant as long as the belief is strong enough. Hence faith.

Great beauty has emerged in the various forms that Christianity, for example, has employed to promote its message. The exquisitely moving choral traditions, the thoughtful liturgical variations, the beautiful work of the monastic scribes let alone the inspirational Churches, Cathedrals and Monastic buildings.

Many choose to take the guidance to follow a 'good' life, others do not. Mafia bosses were often deeply Catholic, but it didn't impact on their behaviour towards others outside their intimate family groups. Belief therefore is vulnerable to the extremes of human 'wants'. It can become dangerously dogmatic. One only has to remember the exploits of the medieval Crusaders, 1095-1291, sanctioned by papist decrees. Encouraged by religious fervour they were responsible for many massacres of both Muslim and heretical Christians. The death toll during those two hundred years has been estimated to be between 2 and 6 million. History is littered with depressingly common religious wars or rivalries.

Whilst reading about these events and being reminded of the appalling suffering engendered by them, I remembered something I saw written on one of the large billboards which are often erected outside churches, particularly if they are roadside, proclaiming some biblical advice. I forget where this was but it read 'Christ died for our sins' and some bright spark had written underneath in equally large letters 'So have many others, mate'.

About 50 years ago, whilst working for Oxfam in Peru on a pottery project for the Amuesha Indians I met a photographer who'd been cataloguing the appalling behaviour of an American evangelical outfit who were destroying the lives of Jungle tribes many of whom had had no contact with the outside world. This outfit called The New Tribes Mission would fly over the jungle to pinpoint a tribal community, then send out parties to forcibly bring them back to the mission base so they could be introduced to God otherwise they would go to hell! In doing so, some died from western diseases, others were so disorientated either from the loss of their own culture or the loss of a loved one, that they became depressed or turned to drink. Those who did survive either became tame Indians to help with the evangelical work or fed the factories being built near the mission stations. The Mennonite missionaries, since the 1920s were not without blame in carrying out similar activities.

Heraclitus, the Greek philosopher who lived around 500 BC, said that religion was a disease, but a noble one. In this case there was no compassion, no nobility. At least there was an empathetic Catholic missionary, expelled from Paraguay in 1976, who said 'leave them in peace in their own land, leave them in peace so that they can decide for themselves what cultural traits they want to change, leave them in peace so that they can continue to be different.'

On returning to England, the photographer put on what was intended to be an educational show of the harrowing photographs he took of the Mission's activities whilst in Paraguay. I went to see the exhibition at the ICA in London but halfway through the opening, agents, we could only assume from the British Government, came in and closed the show down. The exhibition had been sponsored by Survival International and the Paraguay committee for Human Rights, Oxfam, Christian Aid, the Catholic Fund for Oversees Development, the Contemporary Archive on Latin America, the Centre of Concern for Human Dignity, the Catholic Institute for International Relations and Amnesty International. My guess was that the Government didn't want any adverse publicity concerning Paraguay due to some trade deal that was going down.

So belief, as dogma, creates conflict. Entrenched thinking becomes inflexible and discourages innovative enquiry as the Church feels more and more that it is a custodian of traditional teaching. The protection of the teaching becomes paramount and the truth or truths that that teaching points to, are obscured and new thinking is discouraged. The forms become more important than the essence. The often beautiful and impressive but extravagant buildings, the opulent and ostentatious vestments, the rituals, the penances, the cultural attendances with all the accompanying paraphernalia that that entails, become paramount. And all those trappings and paraphernalia required for the administration and promotion of belief are strengthened and predicated on its unprovability.

An example that is often cited to illustrate this entrenchment is the case of Copernicus, the sixteenth century astronomer, who worked out that the Sun was the centre of our solar system, and not as previously thought, the Earth. He even delayed the publication of his book for fear of the Church's reaction as this new truth was clearly opposed to the orthodox view. Galileo, in supporting Copernicus's findings was deemed heretical by the Catholic Church and imprisoned. He was only released after admitting his error, tongue in cheek no doubt.

Later the Church was similarly unnerved by Darwin's evolutionary theory of Natural Selection. Although the Church had no official stance against the idea of evolution, there was much theological opposition to his theory as it conflicted with the biblical account of creation. Today, particularly in America, creationism is commonly taught amongst fundamentalist Christian's who are in denial of geological and fossil evidence. Jehovah Witnesses think similarly, although they allow some scientific evidence. A lesser-known example is the work of Thomas Fairchild, the first professor of botany at Cambridge University, who, in the 17th century, was the first to hybridise plants. The Church's belief in the immutability of creation was subsequently challenged.

More recently the absurd fatwa against Salman Rushdie is an example of the rigidity of belief in certain sectors of fundamentalist Islam, as are the atrocities by ISIS in Syria and elsewhere. And the Taliban in Afghanistan, because of their extreme interpretation of the Koran, are denying educational and political rights particularly to woman. And recently musical instruments have been publicly burned as the playing of such is considered a 'sin'! The irony is not lost on me that the destruction of such instruments might be considered a greater sin!

In Iran, women are also treated as second class citizens oppressed by discriminating Sharia laws affecting almost all aspects of life from marriage to inheritance and even travel. And this is apart from draconian punishments for theft, blasphemy and adultery. These discriminatory laws are imposed by men for socio-political reasons of power and control. Today they are killing women for not wearing the hijab! The fundamentalist thinking of the supreme leader and the judiciary has been effectively frozen, more or less, from the eleventh century onwards. What are they afraid of? These are just a few examples of religious intolerance across the planet, often stoked by political interests. I'm certain that the originators of the truths that the subsequent beliefs represent, would be horrified at how humanity, usually through the exercise of control, has insanely distorted their teachings that they are now unrecognisable. This is the danger of belief that, when fiercely adhered to, and its edicts wrongly interpreted, it can lead to the curtailment of others' freedoms. So, the freedom to choose by one group is to deny freedom to choose in another. And the right to freely choose is being denied extensively across the world right now, both religiously and politically.

On a different tack, in order to get myself up to speed as it were, I recently read a couple of relatively recent publications which oppose each other. One was Richard Dawkins 'The God Delusion' and the other was the earlier 'Honest to God' by the Anglican Bishop of Woolwich John A.T. Robinson. Both were strongly argued, one for and the other against, a belief in God. 'Honest to God', even though it argued for a belief in God, was highly provocative at the time of publication as it challenged what many bishops thought was lazy and complacent thinking in the theological church community. And clearly the Bishop was a fan of the controversial theologian, Paul Tillich. Richard Dawkins in his recognisably donnish style bravely and strongly attempted to demolish the idea of a God per se. Having ploughed through them both often absorbed and sometimes befuddled by their intellectual rigour, it occurred to me that they were both arguing for their beliefs!

'In conversation my perception's rather fine, I see both points of view, the one that's wrong, and mine.' Unknown.

For Christians, it's customary that you should believe in certain things.
a) That Jesus's mother became pregnant as a virgin
b) That Jesus was the son of God, whatever that means
c) That Jesus performed miracles, events that break the laws of nature.
d) That after crucifixion and death, he came back to life
e) That there is life after death
f) There is a heaven and a hell

A healthy dose of scepticism would be a useful starting point here. In what other area would we accept the thinking of 2,000-year-old scribes? We no longer accept the unscientific explanations by, for example, Galen, a Greek physician and philosopher who was born about 130 years after Jesus died. He had no idea that blood circulated around the body, instead he wrote 'The heart is, as it were, the hearthstone and source of the innate heat by which the animal is governed.' The ancient Greeks considered the pneuma (the breath) to be a mixture of air and fire and also that the lower animals were spontaneously generated from decaying matter! And so on. Given that, at the time, the oral tradition was more prominent than the written word and that the New Testament only started to be written from about 40 years after Jesus died, a pinch of salt as to the veracity of many of the stories, with plenty of time for the then contemporary imagination to embellish is, I think, reasonable.

But let's assume that Jesus, like the Buddha (and maybe a few others throughout history) had a powerful enlightenment experience in which they saw an alternative paradigm, a better way to live, that hadn't been considered or understood before. Naturally they would have wanted to tell others about it but because of the difficulties in describing the ineffable, stories or parables illustrating the underlying truths were employed. So far so good, but humans, who were not in that alternate field of understanding, have over time, misunderstood or misinterpreted what was originally meant and that unfortunately has become main-stream. Truths are scattered throughout religious texts but without the necessary insight, have become obfuscated and barnacled with spurious interpretations which are almost impossible to disentangle from the accompanying verbiage.

'Because it is so unbelievable, the truth often escapes being known.'
  Heraclitus.

There is no doubt that the story of Jesus's life is a powerful one and that there are many who have piously devoted their lives to his teachings over many centuries, but I have to ask ' Has the teaching of the last 2,000 years of Christian, Buddhist, Hindu, Islamic or whatever beliefs fundamentally shifted human behaviour to the level that these pioneers intended?' I think not, given how we collectively continue to think and behave. The planet and many of its people are suffering from a rigidly conventional and un-evolving consciousness. In a song Pink Floyd expressed this as 'comfortably numb' and for many I suspect it might be 'uncomfortably numb'. But what is required is a more open, appropriate, mature and serious behavioural approach to the many problems we presently face which, if not forthcoming, are likely to further impoverish and even endanger the extraordinary life that has evolved on this remarkable and beautiful planet.

Although in past cultures thousands of different Gods have been prayed to and worshipped, the present predominant belief, at least in the West, is a monotheist one. The idea that there is only one God is so deeply endemic in the West that if you want, for example, to be the President of the United States you have to profess to believe in God, or lie if you don't, otherwise you won't get the job! Intercessory or petitionary prayer to such a God is commonplace despite the fact that there is scant evidence of the efficacy of such an activity. Amongst many studies on prayer, the best known one is the STEP project, run by Dr. Herbert Benson in 2006 at the Mind/Body Medical Institute in Boston, U.S.A and the results, if you check them out, were inconclusive.

I remember recently watching the Pope appearing on the balcony of the Vatican overlooking St. Peter's Square and offering prayers to the victims and surviving families of the recent Turkish/Syrian earthquake disaster and I thought 'How is that going to help?' It seems to me that prayer is often a way to absolve oneself of the responsibility to do something constructive or it makes you feel good because you *think* you have done something constructive! And also, why do believers, particularly in affluent societies, continue to worship the God whom they profess to be the God of Creation whilst living an unthinking, destructive and profligate lifestyle which cares little for it? Paying lip service, for example, to environmental concerns by waste recycling doesn't address the massive problem of excessive consumption, one of the main causes of the Earth's vital impoverishment. Worshipping or praying to a God won't cut it. Who in their right mind would want to be worshipped anyway unless they were an arrogant narcissist? Belief systems the world over have done nothing, or at least very little, to address our collective insensitivity to evolution, or if you prefer, Creation. With few exceptions, our general lack of care for other people and the animals and plants with whom we share this planet, prayers or no prayers, worship or no worship, belief or no belief, is clearly evident.

'Nothing is so easy as to deceive oneself, for what we wish, we readily believe.'
   Demosthenes.

7

Art And Creativity

'I love the process of discovery, of letting go, of allowing one's aliveness its own unique play. It's fascinating to watch and be absorbed by this relationship between disciplined technique and the free play of the heart.'

Relating back to a short period of teaching back in the 1980s I was driving into Carlisle to start my day's teaching at the Art College and I was thinking about how to inspire, excite or enthuse a particularly unresponsive bunch of students. I knew that the word inspiration originally came from breathing, literally to draw in breath. All of us I'm sure can recall moments when, on seeing, for example, a range of mountains for the first time, a stunning sunset, a birth, a musical performance, a painting, a pot, or a dance, we involuntarily drew in breath. We inspired, we were inspired. While I was mulling this over, I drove past a municipal building, designed in the '60s, now used as part of the local council offices, an ugly, ill-conceived piece of architecture. I became aware that my chest visibly subsided as I passed. I had 'expired', my breath had been expelled.

So, I thought, why isn't there a word in the English language that expresses the opposite of inspiration since clearly my body in its response had understood? Expiration, that which devitalises, that which subtly, imperceptibly and insidiously deflates the spirit. Particularly in urban environments we are surrounded with much that is ugly, much that is expirational.

Where then do we look for uplifting experiences, nourishment for the heart and mind? In nature certainly, and in the Arts; theatre, music, painting, architecture, pottery, glass blowing, etching, textiles, metalwork, woodwork, instrument making, sculpture, literature, and so on. Given that each of us is open to some of these arts, the communication we receive, at least at first, tends to be felt in the gut, bypassing the intellect. It is real, it is felt, it is experienced. The heart is engaged, not the mind. I am moved, I feel. Later maybe the intellect describes or explains.

The problem for education in the arts is, how does it awaken, enthuse, get through to and sensitise when the overwhelming bias is towards the factual and the descriptive? Education is heavily weighted to that which can be measured, marked and recorded. In our insistence on measurement, are we not missing the 'spiritual' aspects of our being? I use the word spiritual not in the religious sense, not barnacled with moral considerations but more in the sense of our natural spirit, our love of something, our enthusiasm for, our excitement of a, b or c. The word education comes from the Latin 'educare', literally to lead or draw out, referring to the skill of discovering the qualities existing in any given person.

Modern education is often more akin to induction—to cram in, to coerce, to inculcate, not for the betterment of a growing consciousness, not for the purposes of nurturing a young mind to be kind, to be sensitive, to question and to think, but for the acquisition of a job. Notwithstanding the excellent work of many of our often undervalued teachers, quantifications are nevertheless often taking the place of qualifications. Perhaps it's not surprising that teachers have less time to inform today's youth as to how to relate, how to respond, and how to feel in ways which would seed a healthier society.

The word art is derived from the Latin word 'ars' meaning skill or craft. It was first used in the thirteenth century and appeared as art, artefact or artifice. Artifice was the preferred word as the object made, painted or sculpted was not the real thing, therefore artificial. Over the centuries art came to mean a form of expression. In Europe painting, sculpture, opera and ballet became elevated to 'high art' distinguishing it from craft, handmade objects for everyday living. Even today the same distinction is made, mainly due to the high value placed particularly on those paintings and sculptures created by favoured artists. And where there is high value, investment comes into play which further elevates their 'importance'. In Japan attitudes to the creative processes are understood at the level of merit rather than monetary value and they have a wise saying, 'There are no major or minor arts, only major and minor artists'.

Life is creative and expresses itself through form. On this home planet of ours there are millions of diverse forms of animal, plant, fungi, bacteria and viruses all evolved from the extraordinary challenges that nature has had to face. We are one of those forms and our 'life', our vitality, finds its own expression through dance, theatre, literature, painting, sculpture, pottery, music, film, architecture, and so on. Life recognises life.

As a young potter I thought that my enthusiasm and love of pottery would shine through my work. I had certainly been moved by many examples of Tsu Chou, Tang or Sung pots, amongst many others, in the Victoria and Albert Museum in South Kensington. I thought of it as a sort of triangular relationship where one's vitality is somehow transferred to another through form. Michael Cardew, one of the finest exponents of our craft here in England expressed this beautifully in his book, 'The Pioneer Potter'. I have used the word artist instead of potter since what he says works across any expressive activity:

'When an artist not only knows his job but delights in it, when technique and inspiration become identified, the glow of life will begin to appear in his work. Nobody can say in rational terms exactly what this glowing consists of, or how the inanimate can be capable of transmitting life from the maker to the user, but it is a fact of common experience.'

I can't remember whether I was told this by a friend or whether I read it somewhere but J. Krishnamurti, the highly respected Indian teacher was asked at one of his talks 'What is Art?' After a brief pause, he answered

'Putting things in the right place'. At first, I thought this response was a touch facile but on further reflection, I saw a profundity I hadn't initially seen. There is a word in English, 'composition', meaning 'to place with' which reflects this. What great art does is, through strong form, or colour combination, or dance sequence, or musical notation etc, create experiences which can open feeling and evoke a sense of connectedness and love. And our vitality is awakened and touched by putting things in the right combination together. Art's function is to enrich, to keep alive a sense of beauty, to touch feeling as a counter or balance to reason and to educate and inform.

My understanding of the creative process became clearer when I began to think about how we learn. Is there a distinction between intellectual understanding and looking? The former we have already touched on. It is knowledge that is factual, measurable and recordable. An additive and cumulative process that is retrievable through time. It has a focus, it is goal-orientated. Learning through looking turns out to be the complete opposite. We all do it but it is much less obvious. The process is not additive but subtractive. It is error-focused learning; not this, not that. It's goal-oriented in the sense that one wants the painting, the pot, the dance etc, to be as expressive as possible, but in the actual activity of looking the mind needs to be unfocused, waiting for the moment when it, in the case of dance or acting for example, feels 'right'. That choice is made in the immediacy of now, not time based, not measurable. Your own aliveness sees the best choice in that moment of time and it's that aliveness that communicates to the onlooker.

CREATIVITY IN OTHER AREAS

Scientists, engineers, cooks, gardeners etc can all use their creative ability, whether it's for the good of mankind or not. I'm astonished at the complexity of many of the manufacturing processes today. And in my field of ceramics, there are now factories where the clay goes in one end and glazed plates come out the other. No one in the premises apart from an overseer in the computer controlling room. The final product may not be aesthetically pleasing but the creative ingenuity that has gone into the design of such a place, is impressive. Someone has had to design the machines that make such productivity possible. How do machines pick and shell peas without damaging them? How have the engineers come up with robots to put cars together on the production lines? Or to make space rockets and landers, or to miniaturise circuit boards in phones, or to work out complex GPS systems for missiles and launch accuracy? These activities require extraordinary ingenuity and creative thought. It may not be the best use of our minds for the latter; but they are unfortunately necessary in our present vulnerable and unstable times.

However, given these times in which we live, the climate emergency, mass migration, overpopulation, resource depletion, wars, thoughtless economic policies and so on, we have to ask; Is there any evidence that all this extraordinary artistic endeavour and engineering creativity is improving our awareness and our responsibility to ourselves and our planet? After all creative people are supposed to see more sensitively and feel more profoundly. Or are our activities just another expression of self-indulgence, of selfishness, even if we have to get out of the way to better express our vitality? We have, and still are, creating moving performances in music and theatre and producing works of great beauty in many fields of expression, some of political or environmental relevance. Works, like Banksey's for example are making us more aware of social and political problems. But awareness in itself is not enough, awareness isn't action. In the great scheme of things, my own creativity has no great transforming significance. Others may be inspired by the beauty made possible from such an activity or deeply touched by the feelings it can engender. Or it may encourage a student to commit to a life engaged in making a creative living but it won't help much in helping us to shift to a more mature consciousness, a mature consciousness in which dilemma is progressively minimised. And for those of us who are in a position to do so, we will need to learn to give more and want less.

Apart from life's immense ability to be creative, it's important to realise that life is innocent—it asks nothing, allows everything—and as we've seen, is often abused but doesn't complain. It has created, evolved and taken care of us and all life for long aeons of time, so using its gift to serve ourselves rather than enhance and enrich the planet which conceived us, is disrespectful and unkind. Each of us needs to use our creativity, whether we inhabit a creative field or not, to find a way to give back, to enhance and to act in appreciation and gratitude for our existence, our being, our extraordinary life. The art of living is perhaps the greatest of all arts, but as yet, the least understood.

8

The Possible 'you *and* me' Mindset

'To the extent that you get out of the way do you know truth.'
Thomas Merton, Trappist Monk.

This is the hardest chapter to write. I'm attempting to describe something very real and alive, something essentially ineffable. Like the Indian expression, it'll be like the impossibility of keeping a butterfly in a elephant's cage. The understanding I gained from my unexpected experience is clear to me or at least some of it is clear but describing it is something else. I love the title of a book by a Zen master which captures the difficulty perfectly – 'Selling water by the river'. My experience only lasted a few days. I have no way of knowing how deep it was compared to others. I'm certain though that there are various levels of understanding and enlightenment. I may have joined up some of the dots but certainly not all, and I only want to be as honest as I can be with minimal presumption or embellishment.

The ability to communicate requires words. Words are only descriptive of the real. J. Krishnamurti, the well known Indian teacher kept banging on about this in his phrase 'the description isn't the described'. In Zen the phrase 'the finger pointing at the moon, isn't the moon', expresses the same truth. Alan Watts an early member of Zen Buddhism in England decided to travel to America and teach Zen to anyone who was interested. He said later that he took a signpost but people clambered up the signpost rather than follow in the direction it pointed. The development of conceptual language allows us to imagine and to give names to things. But as soon as we name something it then takes on a different reality, a conceptual representation. All our communicating with words can only point to an understanding, it can't realise it. You cannot say what the real is, only what it's not. So it's understandable that stories, parables or fables are used to help in this effort.

Listen to what Lao Tse, a 6th century BC Chinese monk, wrote succinctly in the *Tao Te Ching*:

The Tao that can be told is not the eternal Tao
The Name that can be named is not the eternal Tao

The unnameable is the eternally real
Naming is the origin of all particular things

Free from desire you realise the mystery
Caught in desire you only see the manifestations.

Simply put, behind everything we know, behind our thoughts, our wants, our beliefs, our art, our literature, our theatre, our dance, and so on is an unseen foundational reality (the Tao) that gives rise to all expression through form, creative or otherwise. It is Life, it asks nothing, allows everything, it simply is. Paradoxically this ground of being, to give it another name, is inseparable from form. They are the two sides of the same coin.

The Prajnaparamitra sutra states '*Form is emptiness and the very emptiness is form.*'

I think there are times when many, at more open moments in their lives, have sensed this more foundational reality but maybe because of our long history of thinking that the only explanation for this insightful sensation is a religious one and that somehow a Creator is involved, we are drawn into thinking that that foundational reality is separate from us. That the Creator is separate from us. But look at the Judaic meaning of their word for God, Jahweh, – it means 'I am'. Look at what God is supposed to have said to Moses in Exodus ch.3 v.14, 'I am that I am'. Pointing to what? 'I am' is present tense, it's about '*being*' or what Meister Eckhart, the medieval German mystic, called '*isness*'. God has long been thought of as a separate being, and maybe a controlling entity. My experience says otherwise, that what is being referred to is simply the energy of Life, the Life force which animates but doesn't direct us. It doesn't make rules. It asks nothing, and allows everything. It is present *now* in us. It is simply my being, my 'I am'.

The '*and*' is the operative word here, it implies indivisibility, oneness, not separateness. Iain Scott, in his book 'Human Potential', profoundly and unequivocally states, '*The idea of separateness comes from ignorance, conditioning and presumption. It is a lie. You all perpetuate this self-deceit, individually and collectively. It is true that you have a body that is independent from other bodies and that you each uniquely express your individuality - but you are not separate. You have never known actual separateness. Imagined it, yes. Presumed it, yes. Acted on the presumption of it, yes.*'

The very thing that was clear to me was that there is a force, an energy called 'life'. It was the golden light shimmering along the branches of the weeping larch, through the flower beds, in the grass, and incredibly, in the stones lining the path albeit minimally. It was a few minutes before I realised that it was my 'life force' too. That all life *is* one. An eternal alive nowness expressing itself through form. Unnameable, mysterious and real, but not separate.

Let's try a visual analogy. Sometime ago I was sorting through my CD collection and came across Pink Floyd's 'Dark Side of the Moon' album cover. On it a white light shines into a prism which refracts the light into its constituent colours. In my mind the prism represents the brain and all the colours represent the content of that brain, all the different tendencies and thought processes, reactions, hopes and fears etc., that nature and nurture have provided for any one individual. In our daily lives we interact with the 'colours' of other's, which is equivalent to saying we interact with the 'content' of each other's consciousnesses. We are so caught up in the content that we fail to appreciate the thing that animates the whole shebang, the white light, that is, the unseen energy of Life itself, the formless. What is visible, what is known, is form. I am reminded of the little bird that died in mid flight and landed near to me close to a hedge. You could take that little body, dissect it, get to know the intricacies of its form, its construction, its chemistry, it's bones, blood vessels, feathers and so on enough to write several factual volumes. But the thing that allowed it 'to be' was gone. Life, that mysterious entity, like the parrot in the Monty Python sketch, was no more.

So, form and life are inseparable. Behind form is the formless. Behind the noise of consciousness is silence. Given this central understanding that there is an undivided field, a oneness behind everything, every form, which is beyond adequate description, the question then arises is, 'so what?' Of what practical use is such an understanding? How can this affect a significant maturation in our behaviour towards one another, other manifestations of life and our home planet such that we can become carers, not significant vandals? Well in itself, not much. But it points to a possibility, that humanity hasn't finished in its evolution, that it is still in a relatively immature stage, that we have much, much more to give. That the me, me, me or take, take, take selfish mindset can be changed. It will take time, effort and intention.

A conundrum: *'What gets bigger the more you take away from it?'*

Dissatisfaction is often the trigger to begin to examine oneself. It certainly was in my case. One notices that many things are pleasurable for a while but once that wears off, some other pleasing thing or activity has to take its place. In other words, without continuous pleasurable stimulation to fill us up as it were, with food or retail therapy or gambling or drink, or streaming films and many other forms of activity and entertainment etc., there is a sense of incompleteness, a void which needs to be filled again and again. Contentment seems to be an illusory commodity dependent on pleasurable activities ad infinitum. This 'me' needs to be fed. The culture encourages the individual to follow its wants. The original meaning of the word 'individual', according to one etymological source is '*undivided, integral, whole*', which is opposite to the way we generally use the word these days. I know of few individuals who could be described as such. Most, including myself, would most likely be described as 'dividuals'!

One begins to realise that this 'me', this insatiable self, is the source of pain, of suffering. Not being able to get what one wants ranges from slightly annoying to throwing tantrums. And it's easy to blame others for one's distress rather than looking at one's own behaviour. And the self is really good at avoiding the reality of its re-actions using various defensive strategies to deflect looking at itself.

'*We stand in our own shadow and wonder why it's dark*'.
  Unknown.

Many begin to feel that there must be something more to existence. They may turn to religion for an explanation or one of the many meditation or yoga regimes or temporarily find purpose in conspiracy theories or other minority interests. Often these interests are taken up to avoid the harder job of self-examination. In an earlier chapter I wrote about my early interest in understanding my mind better. And after quieting the untamed noise of consciousness for short moments at first but later for longer periods, one could stand back from the many feral thoughts and begin to ask why they were there, what caused them, had they any relevance to what was happening and so on. Realising that much of the 'noise' was unnecessary, one learnt to let it go. In doing so, a feeling of spaciousness or openness would take its place, like clouds opening up to let a chink of sun through. What gets bigger the more you take away from it? A hole. Letting go of unnecessary content opens up more space to see what else needs dumping accompanied by deeper feeling and openness and so on. Learning to look is an ongoing discipline and becomes exciting and interesting after a while.

At the start of all this, I can remember a couple of minor incidences that gave me a sense that most of my behaviour up to that point in my life had been re-active. Some friends had arrived from town and wanted to go for a walk. My internal reaction was, I don't want to go, but then I decided to ignore that internal want and went anyway. That may seem a very insignificant moment, but it presented a clue as to how not to be re-active to a situation but consciously choosing to be responsive. The other time was the occasion when I was half listening to 'Thought for the Day' on Radio 4. A monk from the Iona community in Scotland was saying that it was important to do what was needed not necessarily what one wanted. I resonated deeply with that thought and took it on board.

As I progressed in a somewhat haphazard unguided way noticing thoughts as they arose during the working day and asking if they were relevant or necessary in the situation and dumping them if not, a spaciousness began to open up encouraging further enquiry.

As the influence of my conditioned self diminished, as I became less the effect of it, an open responsiveness developed. Feelings of inclusiveness deepened and a more unfed contentment began to prevail. As the content of consciousness is examined and its feral nature begins to be understood and tamed, a closer connectivity is felt, a warmth, an increasing opening of the heart. There is a movement away from competition and separateness towards collaboration, consensus, compromise and community. There is a move away from what you want to what is needed. I have not found anywhere a better description of the choice that is necessary to make the shift from a self-centred mindset to a 'service before self' mindset than in Iain Scott's book 'Actions Speak Louder Than Words'.

The Earthshot prize, initiated recently by Prince William, has as its motto 'All for one and one for all'. In our present mindset 'one for all' is a possibility, one person giving themselves for the good of others. Nurses or the military for example. 'All for one' is perhaps a more distant possibility, at least collectively. The only example I can think of that exemplifies this behavioural possibility is a British television programme, D.I.Y SOS: The Big Build, where hundreds of volunteers muck in to help the desperate needs of one family. Imagine a world where that behaviour was normal.

I love the beginning of Eckhart Tolle's book '*A New Earth*' where he imagines the evolution of the flower as closely analogous to the flowering of human consciousness. A few flowers at first but over a long span of time, gradually a widespread flowering, with all the accompanying scents and colours, eventually taking hold.

I had probably previously done enough work on myself for my flowering, my oneness experience to occur but it happened under duress and didn't last long and like the early flowers, conditions weren't right for its continuance. A good friend of mine who knows more about these experiences than I do said that even if you knock out most of the bricks from the psychological prison walls that surround you, they can very easily drift back into place. And this certainly happened in my case. And to make matters worse, because I wasn't honest about my situation at the time, I added many more bricks to the proverbial wall than had been there before! However, the possibility of an evolution to a better consciousness has always stayed with me. The oneness experience is not the end game, it simply happens when the shift to nonself consciousness or other-centredness is advanced enough. It is the beginning of the new. It's when intelligence can finally work for the betterment of the whole and not just the part.

9

As To The Future

At school, when I was about twelve, there was a high wire enclosed, tarmac covered tennis court. The tarmac was beginning to give way to invading plants, particularly thistles, which seemed to have the capacity to push up from underneath, creating cracks. I found the fact that something so soft like a plant had the strength to split a tough material like tarmac, fascinating and confounding. The cracks had encouraged some ants to take up residence and I watched them scurrying around wondering how they managed to organise themselves especially when their home was disturbed. I'm ashamed to say that I sometimes killed ants by bouncing a tennis ball on them as they went about their business. One day I watched two ants seemingly squabbling over a grain of sand. My mind, I'm not sure why, imagined itself to be far away on the surface of Mars, looking down on Earth wondering why it was necessary to squabble. I think that there must have been some emotional tension at home during the holidays and I was trying to make sense of it. The ants had reminded me of my distress at the time.

Remembering this incident recently, I began to wonder how an extraterrestrial might view what we humans are doing to each other and how we are not managing things well. Our profligacy, greed and selfishness in the use of land and resources to supply an exponentially growing and ultimately unsustainable population is impacting other forms of life. Species extinction is at an alarming rate already and our global output of climate changing carbon dioxide, methane and nitrous oxide isn't being addressed with sufficient urgency. We are now consciously reaping what we have already sown. 70 or 80 years ago, no one realised that our collective behaviour was going to have the impact it has had.

Rachel Carson was one of the first people to awaken us to the environmental damage of our activities, focusing on the impact of pesticides, in her ground breaking book 'The Silent Spring'. Later CFCs, chemicals used in refrigeration, were discovered to be destroying the ozone layer which protects us from cosmic rays. Some sheep in the southern tip of South America were found to be going blind because of the rays. But later still I can recall being highly sceptical when I first heard that our activities were affecting the climate, such was the immensity of the idea at the time.

So having created a consumptive society reliant on the use of the easily available 'black gold', there were scientists quite early on calling for the need for restraint or our planet would overheat. The oil companies, protecting their businesses and huge profits dismissed these claims for the next 30 years or so, or were in denial. It is now known that most were aware of the science but when questions arose about climate change, they were quick to parry concerns saying that the science was unproven.

The extraordinary growth in human population, the constant warring factions coupled with the obvious environmental damage and resource use, has further highlighted our behaviour as collectively destructive. So this is the time to seriously challenge our present normally accepted 'you *or* me' mindset. It's not that some people haven't realised the inadequacies of our responses throughout history, but the consequences have never been so in-your-face as they are now. So clearly something has to change. And for anyone who thinks about these things, the extension of our present predicament into the future, without significant change, is extremely worrying. Global warming is likely to lead to more crop failures, more extreme weather events including wildfires, more displacement of people, more water disputes and possibly localised wars. Whilst we may be able to mitigate against the worst of these possibilities, we do have the opportunity to at least attempt to evolve to our full potential.

Some, including top scientists, have suggested that we will at some point have to colonise other planets in our galaxy as we run out of room and resources here. But distances are a problem. The nearest star is Proxima Centauri at 4.2 light years away, which means that light travelling at 186,000 miles a second would take 4.2 years to reach us. Our spaceships are presently capable of about 25,000 miles an hour, five times the speed of an air rifle bullet. At this velocity it would take 80,000 years to reach our nearest star!

Elon Musk has had the idea of sending a metre wide sail made of a thin strong material and once in space it would be punched to its destination by a laser. The claim is that it could quickly reach a fifth of the speed of light. Attached to each corner of the sail would be miniaturised instruments and cameras which could take measurements and pictures as the sail sped past. Even at this suggested speed it would take roughly 25 years to reach the star. So, unless space technology takes a massive step forward, trips to neighbouring planets are simply a pipe dream. 'We have to make it here', the Eagles presciently wrote in one of their songs back in the '70s.

It's always now. And what happens in the future is determined by how we think and act right now both personally and collectively. The conditioning of our consciousness dictates how we think and act in any given circumstance. Our conscious capacity for creative, scientific and social thinking is quite extraordinary but our behaviours often betray that long-evolved capacity by carelessly acting, with the subtlety of a bull in a china shop, when compared with the wonderful complexity of our cellular chemistry which allows and supports that capacity in the first place. Many of our actions are parentally or culturally predetermined and remain unexamined. The present 'you *or* me' mindset is, as we've seen, essentially selfish. Our thoughts and actions are learnt either by watching others or in reaction to hurtful experiences. So the individual 'me' is a unique accumulation of hopes, fears, wants and desires and associated thoughts analogous to the previously mentioned colours refracted from the Pink Floyd prism. These 'colours' make up what psychologists call the psyche. When that psyche becomes disturbed or the suffering is too great, help is required and psychiatrists, psychologists or counsellors are sought.

The skill of these professionals is to find, if possible, where the problem or problems are initiated, whether in childhood or from other traumatic events and bring suppressed, forgotten or avoided experiences into the light of consciousness. This process, if handled sensitively can lead to the release of blocked emotions and/or a deeper understanding helping to transform behaviour and relationships, so that the 'patient' is better able to cope with the vicissitudes of life and its many relationships. But the psyche, the 'me', even if it is now more stabilised, still remains within the field of selfishness. The shift to a nonself consciousness is not known as a viable option, so it isn't pursued.

Some psychologists saw the possibility, Abraham Maslow was one and Carl Jung with his idea of self-actualisation was another. This shift is what I saw as a massive potential in my own 'oneness experience'. There was a wonderfully natural sense of peace and contentment, and a realisation that all life is 'one'. All selfish tendencies are either suspended in a short experience like mine or understood and burnt away in a fuller experience. So, what's left? Pure consciousness, sufficient unto itself, unobscured by selfish concerns, opens up the heart. Compassion (to suffer with) emerges and the need to alleviate the suffering of others becomes obvious. New capacities may need to be learnt in order to function well and be effective in carrying out such work. The 'you *or* me' mindset gradually shifts to a new 'you *and* me' mindset as selfishness is abandoned and 'service before self' becomes naturally established. This possibility only arises when a person deeply realises that most of their thoughts and actions are self-serving.

You may have observed that all the adverts on TV or on social media are encouraging us to buy, better, bigger, more or different. The adverts, almost unfailingly suggest, sometimes subtly, sometimes more blatantly that you'd be a lot happier or sexually more successful if you followed their advice. Or there are constant adverts encouraging us to gamble but to gamble responsibly, pretty much an oxymoron as gambling is hardly a responsible use of money. The gambling industry adverts don't mention the misery of addiction and the occasional suicides engendered by participation in a such risky activity. And it's an industry that is heavily stacked in favour of themselves. Their massive profits allow them to sponsor more and more sporting events giving them greater coverage to attract new gamblers. The cigarette manufacturers used to do the same until they were banned, knowing the harm that smoking did to our health. Is it not time for the legislators to do the same with gambling?

The actions of the advertising industry beg the question 'why are we not already content?', after all, the vast majority of us, in the developed world at any rate, have more than enough clothing, food and shelter. Why keep wanting more or different? Slaves to fashion? Does not this excessively consumptive behaviour disguise our underlying discontent? Even if we get excited with a new kitchen or car (unless one is really needed), it is a relatively short lived pleasure satisfying our need for retail therapy, another indicator of discontent.

Most people would love to earn huge salaries, or win the lottery, or receive large legacies or, the less scrupulous, avoid financial obligations by squirrelling away money in off-shore accounts or in tax free havens. Why? Because we can then get all the things that our society, where money is the main arbiter of success, has taught us to want. In other words we would have the opportunity to enrich ourselves with everything that those riches can offer and to extend our selfishness, to continue to take, take, take. How many, if offered such riches, would be really happy because they could then do something to redress the suffering of others? There are those, even within the spectrum of selfishness who would want that, but very few. The recognition that most of our activities are self-serving, the lack of deep contentment it brings, the conflicts both personal and general it engenders and the way it blocks out a deeper connectivity of feeling, can be the beginning of looking for ways to understand and go beyond the limitations of 'self'. The search for ways to recognise and empty that selfish content have been sought throughout recorded history either through religion or philosophies like Buddhism. I looked for a long time for people who understood what I'd experienced and hadn't interpreted it within a past religious/spiritual context.

If the shift to non-selfishness had been easy, I'm certain it would have happened a long time ago. But like my own 'experience' it occurred in an unexpected, unstructured, unguided and haphazard way. About 25 years ago I came across a small group, The Human Potential Trust,* who know what it takes to make the shift. No hype, no bullshit, straightforward free and structured help. Amongst other educational films, they have recently put out on their YouTube channel a series of 42 short (8 to 12 minute) films guiding anyone interested through the difficulties and pitfalls of such a challenge. I asked the Director of their sister charity 'The Wildlife For All Trust' if they'd chosen to do 42 films as this was the number that was the answer to the Universal Question in the particularly English comedy radio programme 'The Hitchhikers Guide to the Galaxy', adapted from Richard Adams book of the same name. She laughed having not previously made the connection. I would highly recommend anyone seriously interested in making the shift, to take a look at their work.

We are an extraordinary animal, and we have, through the centuries, created amazingly beautiful art, architecture, literature, dance, theatre and so on. And there are some wonderful people in many parts of the world doing their very best in often difficult circumstances to help those less fortunate. We've developed complex scientific understanding in botany, palaeontology, geology, medicine, physics, chemistry, evolution and astronomy. It's a shame that at the very time we are understanding so much about out world, our actions are seriously threatening it. There have been great advances in technology but very little significant advance in the understanding of our own psychology.

We have taken 13.7 billion years to evolve, and self-awareness and intelligence is probably very rare in the universe. Our massive human potential is, at present, for most of us, unimaginable but it's the evolutionary leap that will finally liberate us from, and this can't be expressed enough, the appalling and shameful amount of unnecessary suffering we now bring upon ourselves, other life forms and nature in general. Love and intelligence will finally be able to function for the whole and not just the part and we will no longer continue to sell ourselves far too short. We all have a responsibility to admit our collective failure to adequately care for our home, and to realise that without care we are endangering all life, including our own. Before humans the world was, according to James Lovelock's imagination, 'achingly beautiful'. Do we not owe it to ourselves and our wonderful, vulnerable and precious planetary home, to at least attempt this step, to evolve and mature by choosing to largely give up me-centredness, or selfishness as it is more commonly known, to learn to give and care more and to consume much less - hard and unfamiliar as that might seem?

*www.thehumanpotentialtrust.org

BIBLIOGRAPHY

Ackerman, Jennifer, *Chance in the House of Fate,* Bloomsbury

Arnold, Sir Edwin, *The Light of Asia*, Kegan Paul, Trench, Trübner & Co. Ltd

Bach, Richard, *The Reluctant Messiah,* Bantam Doubleday Bell Publishing Group

Cardew, Michael, *Pioneer Pottery,* Longman, Green & Co

Carson, Rachel, *The Silent Spring,* Houghton Mifflin

Dawkins, Richard, *The God Delusion,* Bantam Press

Dodd, Mike, *An Autobiography of Sorts*, Canterton Books

Eliot, T. S., *Collected Poems,* Faber & Faber

Emmitt, Stephen, *10 Billion,* Penguin

Erlande-Brandenburg, Alain, *Cathedral Builders of the Middle Ages,* Thames & Hudson

Gellatley, Juliet, *The Silent Ark*, Thorsons

Greek, C. MD and Greek, Jean Swingle, DVM, *Sacred Cows and Golden Geese,* Continuum

Hancock, Graham, *Lords of Poverty,* Arrow

Hawken, Paul [ed], *Draw Down,* Penguin

Hill , John Lawrence, *The Case for Vegetarianism,* Roman & Littlefield inc.

Jackson, Tim, *Prosperity without Growth,* Routledge

Krishnamurti, J., *The First and Last Freedom,* Harper [U.S] and Gollanz [UK]

Lovelock, James, *The Revenge of Gaia,* Penguin, Allen Lane

McDonough, W. and Braungart, M., *Cradle to Cradle,* North Point Press

Monbiot, George, *Heat,* Penguin

Robinson, Ken, *Creative Schools,* Penguin

van de Post, Lawrence, *The Heart of the Hunter*, Penguin

Patterson, Charles, *Eternal Treblinka,* Lantern Books

Prizing, W., *Zen and the Art of Motorcycle Maintenance,* William Morrow & Co.

Robinson, John, *Honest to God,* SCM Press

Russell, Peter, *The Global Brain Awakens,* Element Books

Scott, Iain, *Actions Speak Louder Than Words,* HPT Books

Scott, Iain, *Human Potential,* HPT Books

Scott, Iain, *Avoidance Doesn't Work,* HPT Books

Singer, Peter, *Animal Liberation,* Pimlico

Swimme, Brian and Berry, Thomas, *The Universe Story,* Harper Collins

Taylor, Steve, *Extraordinary Awakenings,* New World Library

Tolle, Eckhart, *A New Earth,* Penguin

Watts, Alan, *The Taboo Against Knowing Who You Are,* Souvenir Press Ltd

Wyne-Tyson, Jon, *The Extended Circle,* Cardinal